JOURNAL FOR THE STUDY OF THE OLD TESTAMENT SUPPLEMENT SERIES
279

Editors
David J.A. Clines
Philip R. Davies

Executive Editor
John Jarick

Editorial Board
Robert P. Carroll, Richard J. Coggins, Alan Cooper, J. Cheryl Exum,
John Goldingay, Robert P. Gordon, Norman K. Gottwald,
Andrew D.H. Mayes, Carol Meyers, Patrick D. Miller

Sheffield Academic Press

God, Anger and Ideology

The Anger of God in Joshua and Judges
in Relation to Deuteronomy and the
Priestly Writings

Kari Latvus

Journal for the Study of the Old Testament
Supplement Series 279

Copyright © 1998 Sheffield Academic Press

Published by Sheffield Academic Press Ltd
Mansion House
19 Kingfield Road
Sheffield S11 9AS
England

Printed on acid-free paper in Great Britain
by Bookcraft Ltd
Midsomer Norton, Bath

British Library Cataloguing in Publication Data

A catalogue record for this book is available from the British Library

ISBN 1-85075-922-7

CONTENTS

Preface	7
Abbreviations	9

Chapter 1
INTRODUCTION 11
   1. The Making of DtrG: The History of the Investigation 12
   2. Studies of the Anger of God 21
   3. Textual Basis 25
   4. The Task 26

Chapter 2
ANALYSES OF THE TEXTS IN JOSHUA AND JUDGES 28
   1. Joshua 23: Other Nations 28
   2. Judges 2: Other Gods 36
   3. Judges 3.7-11; 10.6-16: Other Gods 2 41
   4. Joshua 7: Fire and Stones 47
   5. Joshua 22: God between the Parties 54
   6. Joshua 9: Divine Order 64

Chapter 3
THE ANGER OF GOD IN DEUTERONOMY AND IN THE PRIESTLY
WRITINGS 71
   1. The Anger of God in Deuteronomy, 1–2 Samuel
      and 1–2 Kings 71
   2. Hidden Anger among the Main Themes of Deuteronomy 74
   3. The Priestly Writings: Anger in the Postexilic Power
      Struggle 77

Chapter 4
CONCLUSIONS AND IMPLICATIONS 85
   1. The Writing Process 85
   2. The Anger of God 86

An Uncritical Epilogue
IN SEARCH OF THE THEOLOGICAL INTENTION BEYOND
THE ANGER OF GOD   89

Bibliography   95
Index of References   101
Index of Authors   107

PREFACE

The present study is a much-abbreviated version of a doctoral thesis supervised by Professor Timo Veijola, published in Finnish and accepted in 1993 at the University of Helsinki. The essential part of work was done at the University of Göttingen where I had an opportunity to stay in 1986–87 due to the scholarship given by DAAD (Deutsche Akademische Austausdienst). Special thanks belong to the research circle of Göttingen, especially Professor Rudolf Smend, Professor Lothar Perlitt and Dr Hermann Spieckermann (now professor in Hamburg) and Dr Christoph Levin (now professor in Giessen). Their warm sympathy in everyday life and deep knowledge of Old Testament research encouraged me to persevere in an often lonely path of investigation. Special thanks belong to my advisor, Professor Timo Veijola, who guided the research process with extensive knowledge, strict methodological demands and strong theological passion.

Without the financial support of the Biblical Department, one of the Centres of Excellence at the University of Helsinki, the translation and rewriting process would not have been possible. Therefore I have pleasure in expressing my gratitude to Professor Raija Sollamo (Dean of the Theological Faculty), Professor Heikki Räisänen and Professor Timo Veijola.

Younger colleagues and friends, Master of Theology Mika Aspinen, Master of Theology Seppo Sipilä, Dr Matti Myllykoski and Dr Martti Nissinen have shared many essential methodological reflections and given valuable insights to develop the work.

Ms Jenny Daggers has kindly carried the burden of reading the manuscript of a non-English speaker and has made a notable contribution to making the text more understandable.

One new chapter has been added to the English edition (Epilogue) which probably reflects the directions of my theological journey as well as questions raised in my present working environment in the

Diaconia Institute of Higher Education in Finland. Demands upon theology grow from the reality in which we live, from our social, economic and cultural context. This means that in addition to the classical academic view there is a growing need for a contextual approach to rewriting local theologies in Europe, as much as elsewhere.

This study is dedicated to my students in the Lutheran Theological Seminary in Hong Kong (1992–94) who shared with me the moments of finalizing my doctoral thesis and opened new directions for deeper exploration of the relation between theology and (Chinese and also Western) culture. Warm gratitude will always colour my memories of those years.

ABBREVIATIONS

AASF	Annales Academiae Scientiorum Fennicae
AB	Anchor Bible
AEHL	Avraham Negev (ed.), *The Archaeological Encyclopedia of the Holy Land* (Englewood Cliffs, NJ: Prentice–Hall, 3rd edn, 1990)
AnBib	Analecta biblica
AOAT	Alter Orient und Altes Testament
ATD	Das Alte Testament Deutsch
BBB	Bonner biblische Beiträge
BDB	Francis Brown, S.R. Driver and Charles A. Briggs, *A Hebrew and English Lexicon of the Old Testament* (Oxford: Clarendon Press, 1907)
BEATAJ	Beiträge zur Erforschung des Alten Testaments und des Antiken Judentums
BETL	Bibliotheca ephemeridum theologicarum lovaniensium
BHS	*Biblia hebraica stuttgartensia*
BKAT	Biblischer Kommentar: Altes Testament
BWANT	Beiträge zur Wissenschaft vom Alten und Neuen Testament
BZ	*Biblische Zeitschrift*
BZAW	Beihefte zur *ZAW*
ConBOT	Coniectanea biblica, Old Testament
DJD	Discoveries in the Judaean Desert
EdF	Erträge der Forschung
EHAT	Exegetisches Handbuch zum Alten Testament
FRLANT	Forschungen zur Religion und Literatur des Alten und Neuen Testaments
GTA	Göttinger theologische Arbeiten
HALAT	Ludwig Koehler *et al.* (eds.), *Hebräisches und aramäisches Lexikon zum Alten Testament* (5 vols.; Leiden: E.J. Brill, 1967–95)
HAT	Handbuch zum Alten Testament
HKAT	Handkommentar zum Alten Testament
HSM	Harvard Semitic Monographs
ICC	International Critical Commentary
IDB	George Arthur Buttrick (ed.), *The Interpreter's Dictionary of the Bible* (4 vols.; Nashville: Abingdon Press, 1962)
JBL	*Journal of Biblical Literature*
JSOT	*Journal for the Study of the Old Testament*

JSOTSup	*Journal for the Study of the Old Testament*, Supplement Series
KHAT	Kurzer Hand-Kommentar zum Alten Testament
NCB	New Century Bible
OBO	Orbis biblicus et orientalis
OTL	Old Testament Library
OTS	*Oudtestamentische Studiën*
RB	*Revue biblique*
RevQ	*Revue de Qumran*
SAA	State Archives of Assyria
SBS	Stuttgarter Bibelstudien
SESJ	Publications of the Finnish Exegetical Society
SOTSMS	Society for Old Testament Study Monograph Series
StudOr	Studia orientalia
THAT	Ernst Jenni and Claus Westermann (eds.), *Theologisches Handwörterbuch zum Alten Testament* (Munich: Chr. Kaiser, 1971–76)
ThW	Theologische Wissenschaft
VT	*Vetus Testamentum*
VTSup	*Vetus Testamentum*, Supplements
WBC	Word Biblical Commentary
ZAW	*Zeitschrift für die alttestamentliche Wissenschaft*
ZTK	*Zeitschrift für Theologie und Kirche*

Chapter 1

INTRODUCTION

The *Star Wars* trilogy of films, a modern Hollywood myth, connects good and bad, love and anger in the shape of Darth Vader, the evil and dark commander of a spaceship who, despite his mask of anger, was basically good but needed to be saved by his own son Luke (the hero). The trilogy creates a multidimensional, strongly relational and touching story about the fight between good and evil which culminates in the moment when Luke uncovers the mask of his father and finally sees his authentic face. The battle for a good life is a journey beyond the masks; even in the goodness of the hero, anger and revenge are fighting for their place.

This modern myth and the much older one, written by deuteronomistic theologians in the Deuteronomistic History (DtrG), illustrate the need to bind together fundamental elements of life, good and bad, love and anger, hope and judgment. The God of love and mercy in the Old Testament very often turns into the God of anger and punishment. This duality is so ambiguous that it has caused serious objections through the centuries; among others Marcion must be mentioned in this connection. He even launched a theological programme to reject the Old Testament because of its concept of God. According to Marcion's understanding, the God of Jesus, that is, true God, is nothing but good and loving.

This study has been for me a journey mapping the darker side of God: the anger of God in the Old Testament. The concentration on the deuteronomistic writings, particularly on Joshua and Judges, and finally the comparison to the Priestly Writings and Deuteronomy aim at structuring the historical frames, if not origin, of the anger of God in the Old Testament. Wider theological reflection goes beyond the task of the present study but will nonetheless be discussed briefly throughout the study and especially in the epilogue.

The purpose of this study is to analyse how the idea of the anger of God is used in the books of Joshua and Judges in the light of the historical and social environment of the writers. The first task of the study is the analysis of the growing process of the text. How, where and when were the passages related to this theme written? On the grounds of these results it is possible to examine more closely the theological emphasis of different writers and their connections to historical and theological contexts and to compare these results to the other theologically central historical writings in the Old Testament: Deuteronomy and the Priestly Writings.

1. *The Making of DtrG: The History of the Investigation*

The Nineteenth Century

It is possible to define three decisive positions in the history of the investigation of the Deuteronomistic History (DtrG) which have to be taken into consideration. At the end of the nineteenth century the study of the former prophets lived in the shadow of the flourishing pentateuchal source analysis[1] but interest was also shown in the origin of individual books like Joshua and Judges. The existence of deuteronomistic material in those books was commonly recognized,[2] as well as the heterogeneous literary character of the text. The studies of A. Kuenen especially have to be mentioned in this connection. While he was using the pentateuchal patterns also in the area of the former prophets he put particular stress on the deuteronomistic editing (*Bearbeitung*) of the texts which could be found throughout the books.[3]

---

1.   The decisive insight of W.M.L. de Wette (*Dissertatio critico-exegetica qua Deuteronomium a prioribus Pentateuchi libris diversum, alius cuiusdam recentioris auctoris opus esse monstratur* [Jena, 1805] *Beiträge zur Einleitung in das Alte Testament* [Halle, 1806/1807]) was to connect the birth of Deuteronomy with the Josianic reform, i.e. to the late seventh century, so creating a relatively fixed point for new theories explaining the writing process of the Old Testament.

2.   Among others, J. Wellhausen, *Die Composition des Hexateuchs und der historischen Bücher des Alten Testaments* (Berlin: George Reimer, 3rd edn, 1899), pp. 208, 300-301, thought that historical books (Judges–Kings) contained several independent stories which had already found a fixed form before deuteronomistic editing (*Bearbeitung*).

3.   A. Kuenen, *Historisch-kritische Einleitung in die Bücher des Alten Testa-*

Kuenen developed his insight further on and showed that numerous tensions in the content and style are caused by the literary activities of successive redactors.[4] Around the year 600 BCE the dtr-redactor collected a history of kings which covered the plot from the judges to the kings, that is, about the period present in 1–2 Samuel and 1–2 Kings. This text was later supplemented by a deuteronomistic-orientated 'second redactor' who attached large parts of Judges as well as other supplementary material to the existing writing.[5]

Large appendixes (Judg. 1.1-2.5; 17-21; 2 Sam. 21-24) were added at about the same time when the books were divided into smaller units. This was done by the post-deuteronomistic 'canonical redactor' (*der kanonische Redactor*) who worked before the influence of the Priestly Writings, during the first part of the fifth century.[6] Finally, some smaller passages already presuppose the existence of P and must be dated to the latter part of fifth century.[7]

Thus Kuenen offered the opinion that the historical books were not written by a single author but on the contrary they were produced by

---

ments, 1.2 (Leipzig: Schulze, 1890), pp. 99-100: 'Es hat sich uns ergeben, dass die drei Bücher nicht nur hinsichtlich ihres Inhalts sich an einander anschliessen, sondern auch die deuteronomische Bearbeitung eines grossen Theiles des verwendeten Materials mit einander gemein haben. Wir sind zunächst geneigt, diese Bearbeitung, eben weil sie in allen drei Büchern sich zeigt, ein und demselben Autor zuzuschreiben.' It should be noticed that Kuenen continously uses the expression 'deuteronomic' instead of 'deuteronomistic'.

Wellhausen, *Die Composition*, p. 235, was more willing to emphasize the meaning of sources rather than redactors: 'Aber einheitliche schriftstellerische Konceptionen sind die Bücher Samuelis und der Könige dennoch nicht, vielmehr ebenfalls Kompilationen aus verschiedenen Quellen.'

4. Kuenen, *Historisch-kritische Einleitung* (1.2), p. 100: 'Auf die erste deuteronomische Bearbeitung folgte, wie wir gesehen haben, wenigstens in den Büchern Samuelis und der Könige, eine fortgesetzte Diaskeue.'

5. Kuenen, *Historisch-kritische Einleitung* (1.2), pp. 7-12, 100, locates e.g. Judg. 2.6–16.31 to this 'second dtr-redactor'.

6. Kuenen, *Historisch-kritische Einleitung* (1.2), pp. 100-101. In a similar way Wellhausen, *Die Composition*, pp. 235-36, accepts the post-deuteronomistic character of end redaction. 'Wie in den Bb. der Richter und der Könige ist auch im Buch Samuelis die Schlussredaktion nachdeuteronomistisch.'

7. Kuenen, *Historisch-kritische Einleitung* (1.2), pp. 101-103: 'Es steht jedoch fest, dass der Text der Sa[muelis] noch lange nach 450 v. Chr. ergänzt und erweitert worden ist.' We can find similar conclusions also related to the other historical books.

many writers during a long process of literary formation. Even if Kuenen could not modify his thesis in a way which would have achieved consensus among scholars we may estimate his methodological approach as a breakthrough and still very valuable. Sometimes Kuenen's position has been understood rather mechanically, due to his terms 'first' and 'second redaction' as if he were the first representative for the double-redaction model.[8] Such a misinterpretation has grounds in Kuenen's terminology but it should be noticed that 'the second redaction' is not a synonym for a single author or text layer but points to the long and successive phase of the redaction process which includes numerous insertions by different hands.[9]

The Twentieth Century before Martin Noth
When we turn to the twentieth century it is rather easy to notice that two major assumptions were shared widely among scholars. First, the texts of the former prophets were recognized to be more or less non-logical and fragmentary in their literary character; and second, those texts were understood to contain some deuteronomistic material. By putting together a huge number of individual observations along these lines writers of the commentaries spoke about two successive deuteronomistic redactions. The former, always the main text, was dated to the pre-exilic and the latter to the exilic period. The number of texts belonging to the exilic writer were evaluated as so small that he became merely a minor modifier of the text with his small insertions.[10]

8. F.M. Cross, *Canaanite Myth and Hebrew Epic: Essays in the History of the Religion of Israel* (Cambridge, MA: Harvard University Press, 2nd edn, 1975), p. 275; R. Nelson, *The Double Redaction of the Deuteronomistic History* (JSOTSup, 18; Sheffield: Sheffield Academic Press, 1981), pp. 14-16; and partly also E. Würthwein, *Die Bücher der Könige: 1. Kön. 17–2. Kön. 25* (ATD 11.2; Göttingen: Vandenhoeck & Ruprecht, 1984), p. 486.

9. Kuenen, *Historisch-kritische Einleitung* (1.2), p. 96: 'Von der zweiten Redaction bezw. Ueberarbeitung der Königsbücher, deren Umfang und Verhältniss zu der ersten wir im bisherigen festzustellen versuchten, kann man nicht annehmen, dass sie zu ein und derselben Zeit und von ein und derselben Autor bewirkt worden ist. Auch hier drängt sich uns, ebenso wie beim Hexateuch und den Büchern Samuelis, mit Nothwendigkeit die Vorstellung von einer fortgesetzten Diaskeue des Textes auf.'

10. I. Benzinger, *Die Bücher der Könige* (KHAT, 9; Freiburg: J.C.B. Mohr, 1899), pp. xiii-xv (R^1 between 621 to 597, R^2 exilic); R. Kittel, *Die Bücher der Könige* (HKAT, 1.5; Göttingen: Vandenhoeck & Ruprecht, 1900), p. viii (Rd soon

A different approach was represented by those who tried to solve the literary questions of the former prophets by applying Pentateuchal source criticism. Even when researchers like K. Budde, O. Eissfeldt and G. Hölscher made several valuable observations their basic hypotheses relating to J- and E-sources were not accepted by the majority of scholars.[11]

Another essential position is worth mentioning. C. Steuernagel shares with his contemporaries a lot of common knowledge about the heterogeneous and deuteronomistic character of the text. His peculiarities become more obvious when we study his theories about the redaction. Even when he does not handle all the former prophets as a single literary block his basic solutions of the books follow the same pattern. They all have more or less pre-deuteronomistic early forms or sources which have been modified and supplemented by dtr-redactors Rd^1 and Rd^2. Also some post-deuteronomistic insertions can be found. The most significant point in Steuernagel's assumption is, however, that Joshua and other books of former prophets contained so many different insertions that they must not be understood as a work of one or two individuals but as the work of a collective group (*ein Kollektivum*).[12]

Finally, Steuernagel drew a few lines to give a shape to the larger deuteronomistic editing process (*Bearbeitung*). The first redactor collected his sources based on his deuteronomistic principles, thus creating a story from Solomon to Josiah. In about the year 600 it was supplemented with Joshua-stories, and during the exile with Judges and some parts of Kings. Steuernagel classifies the postexilic additions inserted into the Deuteronomistic History (*dtn. Geschichtswerk*) as a separate group.

As a matter of fact, the general lines of Kuenen and Steuernagel

after 600, R exilic but after 561); W. Nowack, *Richter, Ruth* (HKAT, 1.4.1; Göttingen: Vandenhoeck & Ruprecht, 1900), pp. iv-v (redactor Rd followed by post-deuteronomistic Rp); A. Šanda, *Die Bücher der Könige I–II* (EHAT, 9.1; Münster: Aschendorff, 1911/1912), pp. xxxvi-xli (R after 587, Rj after 560).

11. R. Smend, *Die Entstehung des Alten Testaments* (ThW, 1; Stuttgart: W. Kohlhammer, 2nd rev. edn, 1981), p. 111; J.H. Hayes, *An Introduction to Old Testament Study* (Nashville: Abingdon Press, 2nd edn, 1980), pp. 202-206.

12. C. Steuernagel, *Das Deuteronomium: Das Buch Josua* (HKAT, 1.3; Göttingen: Vandenhoeck & Ruprecht, 1900), pp. 144-45. See also the summaries at the end of the analysis of individual books in C. Steuernagel, *Lehrbuch der Einleitung in das Alte Testament* (Tübingen: J.C.B. Mohr, 1912).

reinforce one another while retaining their own characteristics. Both agree on the successive and long-term writing process, though Kuenen concentrates more on the smaller details, while Steuernagel pays attention also to the general lines.

Martin Noth and his Followers
Martin Noth gave an essentially new impulse to the investigation with his thesis that the books from Deuteronomy to Kings form an independent history edited by the deuteronomistic redactor. The redactor was not described as a free and imaginative storyteller but more like a collector (*Sammler*) who selected and assorted different kinds of tradition. Noth, however, also uses the term 'author' (*Autor*) to mean that the redactor finally created a historical story with a continuing plot.[13]

According to Noth, Deuteronomistic history formed a literary unity which had a unifying historical and theological keynote. By emphasizing the unity of the work Noth clearly opposes the mainstream of his predecessors who were convinced about the heterogeneous, literary character of the text. This surprising difference was not based on different kinds of observations but rather on his willingness to sell his main product—Deuteronomistic history—and ignore less important details. Such an attitude is obvious, for example, when Noth analyses Joshua 23 to Judg. 3.6 and finds several literary layers from the text but ignores them. Also evident to Noth was the existence of the priestly and post-deuteronomistic material. Therefore, it seems that Noth was overreacting when he was speaking about a single redactor, especially when we know that his own occasional observations were pointing to a more complicated redactional process.[14]

Among the scholars Noth's hypothesis about Deuteronomistic history—*one work, one redactor*—was accepted so unanimously that it nearly paralysed all other points of view for a few decades. Remembering the background that in the beginning of this century mainstream scholars were convinced of the existence of double redaction, it is surprising that the work of A. Jepsen about the multi-layer redaction of Kings was left in the shadow of ignorance.[15]

13. M. Noth, *Überlieferungsgeschichtliche Studien: Die sammelnden und bearbeitenden Geschichtswerke im Alten Testament* (Tübingen: Max Niemeyer Verlag, 3rd edn, 1967).
14. About Josh. 23 to Judg. 3 see Noth, *Überlieferungsgeschichtliche*, pp. 7-9, and about priestly material see pp. 188-89.
15. A. Jepsen, *Die Quellen des Köningsbuches* (Halle: Max Niemeyer Verlag,

1. Introduction

As a matter of fact, Jepsen's striving to define redactional layers more carefully was a logical follow-up to the achievements of the earlier researchers. He dated the basic text formed by R^I to the beginning of the sixth century (about 580). Using a chronicle of the kings and the source about building the temple, the writer constructed a critical description of the history of the cult without making any connections with Deuteronomy. This document was redacted by exilic writer R^{II} who gave deuteronomistic colouring to the Kings. Finally, in the postexilic period so-called Levitic redaction (*die levitische Redaktion*) introduced a few texts orientated along the lines of Chronicles. The last-mentioned texts reflected the questions of Levitic priests related to the second temple.

Although Jepsen's results were not accepted by other scholars he pointed out problematic features of the one-writer model: the text of the Deuteronomistic History is too heterogeneous to be produced by a single writer. Jepsen's precise shape of the multilayer model was rejected but his paradigm of successive redactors later showed its importance in the writings of F.M. Cross ('double redaction') and in the Göttingen school (DtrH-DtrP-DtrN).

F.M. Cross argued for the existence of two separate theological themes discernible within the Deuteronomistic History. In the main it is a question of 'the juxtaposition of the two themes, of threat and promise' indicating the work of two redactors. According to Cross the first edition of the Deuteronomistic History was written during the reign of king Josiah and supplemented during the exile by the later redactor who focused his message to exiles on the need for 'repentance' and the promise of 'restoration'. Further, the post-Josianic historical material at the end of Kings belonged to the exilic redactor, although there was no 'theological reflection' as in the other part of the supplementary layer.[16]

Practically Cross did not create a new paradigm but copied the general agreement of critics during the pre-Noth era, simply giving a slightly remodified shape to older concepts without reflecting explicitly the history of research. He mentions briefly how 'the older literary critics... argued for two editions' and concludes that 'we need not

---

1953). Actually the study was complete by 1939 but publishing was postponed because of the war.

16. Cross, *Canaanite Myth*, pp. 274-89.

review here the variety of views nor their specific arguments'.[17]

This model was accepted widely among Anglo-Saxon critics and developed further especially by R. Nelson (1981),[18] A.D.H. Mayes (1983)[19] and I. Provan (1988).[20] While others followed more strictly the pattern of just two writers Mayes opened the view to multidimensional direction and spoke about an 'ongoing process' of interpretation. Characteristics of the later editor can be found in the topics related to obeying the law and the criticism against other gods. Besides these two editorial layers Mayes finds some other insertions and, importantly, argues that a significant part of the text is identified with the post-deuteronomistic period.[21]

Simultaneously in Germany the so-called Göttingen school had developed a redaction model, where the writing process of the Deuteronomistic History was explained with the idea of three successive redactors. At least R. Smend (1971),[22] W. Dietrich (1972)[23] and T. Veijola (1975; 1977)[24] can be counted as belonging to the earliest period of this school. Smend named the literary supplementary layer in the book of Joshua according to its nomistic stress DtrN (N = nomistic). Besides the law theme, warnings against other nations in the land or the worship of their idols were decisive for identifying DtrN-texts. Thus Smend built his hypothesis on two methodological assumptions: first, some texts are later insertions to the basic text (DtrH); and

17. Cross, *Canaanite Myth*, p. 275.
18. Nelson, *The Double Redaction*.
19. A.D.H. Mayes, *The Story of Israel between Settlement and Exile: A Redactional Study of the Deuteronomistic History* (London: SCM Press, 1983).
20. I.W. Provan, *Hezekiah and the Books of Kings: A Contribution to the Debate about the Composition of the Deuteronomistic History* (BZAW, 172; Berlin: W. de Gruyter, 1988).
21. Mayes, *The Story*, pp. 21, 137.
22. R. Smend, 'Das Gesetz und die Völker: Ein Beitrag zur deuteronomistischen Redaktionsgeschichte', in H.W. Wolff (ed.), *Probleme biblischer Theologie* (Festschrift G. von Rad; Munich: Chr. Kaiser Verlag, 1971), pp. 494-509.
23. W. Dietrich, *Prophetie und Geschichte: Eine redaktionsgeschichtliche Untersuchung zum deuteronomistischen Geschichtswerk* (FRLANT, 108; Göttingen: Vandenhoeck & Ruprecht, 1972).
24. T. Veijola, *Die ewige Dynastie: David und die Entstehung seiner Dynastie nach der deuteronomistischen Darstellung* (AASF, Series B, 193; Helsinki: Academia Scientiarum Fennica, 1975); and *idem*, *Das Königtum in der Beurteilung der deuteronomistischen Historiographie: Eine redaktionsgeschichtliche Untersuchung* (AASF, Series B; Helsinki: Academia Scientiarum Fennica, 1977).

second, among these text themes law, other nations and their idols connected them to a single author. On the other hand, Smend was open to acceptance of some redactional activities *after* the work of DtrN but still belonging to the deuteronomistic circle.

This concept was complemented by Dietrich in Kings with an idea of insertions which were later than DtrH but earlier than DtrN. Such texts were mostly connected with prophetic content or had connections to the prophetic literature: the redactor was named DtrP (P = prophetic). In these texts Dietrich saw a special theological emphasis on causality between the acts and the effects. A similar tripartite redaction model was applied in Samuel and Judges by Veijola.

Even if the earliest works of the Göttingen school can be criticized as sometimes too mechanical, division of texts into three categories definitely showed the complex character of the writing process—a viewpoint that was underestimated in the model of double redaction. Through their work the idea of successive writers, each building on predecessor texts, has been widely recognized.

In the 1980s the model of the Göttingen school was modified with regard to the DtrN-layer. Nomistic additions were no longer understood to be the work of a single editor but rather of a group of redactors who were working in succession to one another (Smend,[25] Veijola,[26] Würthwein[27]). Further, the so-called prophetic redactor DtrP was explained as being more like a collective circle (*Kreis*) of writers (Würthwein).[28] On the other hand, the DtrP-hypothesis has turned out to be problematic because in the books of Joshua and Judges scholars have found only a few traces of DtrP.[29]

---

25. Smend, *Die Entstehung*.
26. T. Veijola, *Verheissung in der Krise: Studien zur Literatur und Theologie der Exilzeit anhand des 89. Psalms* (AASF, Series B, 220; Helsinki: Academia Scientiarum Fennica, 1982).
27. Würthwein, *Die Bücher* (1984).
28. Würthwein, *Die Bücher* (1984), pp. 496-98.
29. Among the proposals to find DtrP in the first part of DtrG are worth mentioning Dietrich, *Prophetie,* p. 132 (1 Sam. 2.27-36); Veijola, *Die ewige,* p. 43 (1 Sam. 3.11-14; 28.17-19aα); F. Foresti, *The Rejection of Saul in the Perspective of the Deuteronomistic School* (Studia Theologica, Teresianum 5; Rome: Edizioni del Teresianum, 1984), pp. 176, 180 (1 Sam. 15; 1 Sam. 28 partly); L. Schwienhorst, *Die Eroberung Jerichos: Exegetische Untersuchung zu Josua 6* (SBS, 122; Stuttgart: Verlag Katholisches Bibelwerk, 1986), p. 99 (Josh. 6.21b, 24a, 26).

Compare also the limitation made by Smend, *Die Entstehung*, p. 125: 'Während

Recently Veijola has tried to modify the DtrN-thesis by creating a new sign DtrB (*Bund*) for those texts which are rather close to DtrN but are more related to the covenant theme. Until now Veijola has used the DtrB sign only in Deuteronomy.

Special interest was also paid by Würthwein to those passages which were certainly later insertions but did not contain any deuteronomistic signs. Dating this material to the post-deuteronomistic period Würthwein revived the ideas earlier expressed by Wellhausen and Kuenen. On similar grounds U. Becker[30] has underlined efforts of the Priestly Writings-oriented editor who also belongs to the category of post-deuteronomistic writers.

Methodologically, one of the most remarkable challenges to the Göttingen school was given by C. Levin[31] who introduced a new kind of paradigm which is a creative synthesis of the ideas of Kuenen, Noth and Zimmerli.[32] Levin accepts the existence of the basic-text (DtrH) but is not willing to identify other redactional layers which would continue through the whole Deuteronomistic History. Instead of redactions or redactional levels Levin speaks about smaller insertions or a continuing rewriting process (*Fortschreibung*) where a huge number of additions can be noticed and sorted using relative chronology in one passage without any possibility of identifying them clearly enough for the creation of redactional layers through the DtrG. A corresponding approach is used by McKane[33] in Jeremiah where he used the term 'rolling corpus' to describe the gradual growth of the texts.

Obviously, the vast majority of scholars agree about the heterogeneous or fragmentary character of the text in the Deuteronomistic History. Opinions differ on what kind of disturbances to the coherence

---

DtrH mit Dtn 1 eingesetzt zu haben scheint, ist die Thematik von DtrP begrenzter; sie reicht kaum über die Königszeit zurück.'

30. U. Becker, *Richterzeit und Königtum: Redaktionsgeschichtliche Studien zum Richterbuch* (BZAW, 192; Berlin: W. de Gruyter, 1990).

31. C. Levin, *Der Sturz der Königin Atalja: Ein Kapitel zur Geschichte Judas im 9. Jahrhundert v. Chr* (SBS, 105; Stuttgart: Verlag Katholisches Bibelwerk, 1982); *idem*, 'Joschija im deuteronomistischen Geschichtswerk', *ZAW* 96 (1984), pp. 351-71.

32. W. Zimmerli, *Ezechiel* (BKAT, 13.1-2; Neukirchen–Vluyn: Neukirchener Verlag, 1969).

33. W. McKane, *A Critical and Exegetical Commentary on Jeremiah. I. Introduction and Commentary on Jeremiah I–XXV* (ICC; Edinburgh: T. & T. Clark, 1986).

or integrity of the text one should allow.³⁴ Even if agreement in some cases were possible, the debate among scholars will continue about how and where to set the line between unity and disunity. In a similar way the distinction between redactional layers and an ongoing rewriting process seems to be methodologically an unsolved enigma at this moment.

The history of the investigation with its variety of solutions challenges present work. The main task of the writing process can be focused in the following questions. Is it possible to recognize and identify redactional activities among those texts which handle the anger of God? What is the best way of outlining the growth of the text: double or triple redaction versus ongoing writing process?

Answers to these questions will open the way for the following level of work: dating the anger theme and identifying the of socio-cultural background.

2. *Studies of the Anger of God*

A similar approach has not been used in earlier studies which concentrate on the theme of the anger of God in the Old Testament, and even among the shorter writings there is not a single article that pays attention to the anger theme using a diachronic approach.

Some writings are certainly worth mentioning here. In 1924 P. Volz studied the demonic aspects of Yahweh showing that the concept of God in the Old Testament includes also its dark side. According to Volz God can be described by using expressions like 'fear', 'cruelty', 'destructive', and so on. Such understanding grows from the texts where God without any clear reason attacks Moses (Exod. 4.24), Uzzah (2 Sam. 6.7) or the Israelites (2 Sam. 24.1). Volz underlines that in these passages God's behaviour cannot be explained as a punishment for sins or a reminder of God's holiness, but they show the irrationality that belongs to the concept of God throughout the Old Testament, not only in the primitive phase of religion.³⁵

Regarding the theological and historical background of Volz's presentation two things must be mentioned. At about the same time R. Otto³⁶ focused on the concept of God in his research about the

---

34. Schwienhorst, *Die Eroberung*, pp. 19-20.
35. P. Volz, *Das Dämonische in Jahwe* (Tübingen: J.C.B. Mohr, 1924).
36. R. Otto, *Das Heilige: Über das Irrationale in der Idee des göttlichen und sein*

holy. Both Volz and Otto carried in their texts the historical background of World War I which had in a very concrete way showed the demonic side of the world but also raised interest in transcendence and God's holiness.

A short article written by H. Ringgren[37] in the Festschrift of A. Weiser tried to prove that in ancient Israel there was a covenant festival which included oracles against foreign nations. According to Ringgren God's anger played an important role in this cultic context. The entire structure was based, however, on such hypothetical assumptions about covenant festivals that it lost its meaning.

C. Westermann too concentrated on prophetic literature, analysing the function of the anger of God (an article in the Festschrift dedicated to H.W. Wolff).[38] Westermann pointed out that the anger of God was mostly directed against the Israelites and was always a reaction (mostly to disobedience or the worship of other gods). Further, he underlined that the anger was timely and historically limited. According to Westermann the anger of God is connected in prophetic literature with the major changes of history where God opens new doors in the life of the Israelites through his purifying judgment. Thus the anger becomes a synonym for judgment which has clear and not 'irrational' (Volz) grounds. The decisive point of view in the prophetic literature is that God's grace is superior to anger.

The brief writing of D.J. McCarthy (in memorial writings dedicated to J.P. Hyatt)[39] should not be passed over, as, according to the title, it relates the anger theme to the Deuteronomistic History, and even more so, to its structure and unity. His main thesis is that the Deuteronomistic History contains anger formulae which are basic

Verhältnis zum Rationalen (Breslau: Trewendt und Granier, 9th edn, 1922).

37. H. Ringgren, 'Einige Schilderungen des göttlichen Zorns', in E. Würthwein and O. Kaiser (eds.), *Tradition und Situation: Studien zur alttestamentlichen Prophetie* (Festschrift A. Weiser; Göttingen: Vandenhoeck & Ruprecht, 1963), pp. 107-13.

38. C. Westermann, 'Boten des Zorns: Der Begriff des Zornes Gottes in der Prophetie', in J. Jeremias and L. Perlitt (eds.), *Die Botschaft und die Boten* (Festschrift H.W. Wolff; Neukirchen–Vluyn: Neukirchener Verlag, 1981), pp. 147-56.

39. D.J. McCarthy, 'The Wrath of Yahweh and the Structural Unity of the Deuteronomistic History', in J.L. Crenshaw and J.T. Willis (eds.), *Essays in Old Testament Ethics* (J. Philip Hyatt in Memorium; New York: Ktav, 1974), pp. 97-110.

1. *Introduction*   23

theological concepts and occur in a similar form throughout the work and also confirm the structural and literal unity of Deuteronomistic History:

> To sum up, we find that the wrath theme works in the formation of a well-knit structure in the deuteronomistic history... It is differentiated, not as haphazard collection, but as a meaningful, nuanced construction (p. 106).

A positive attitude towards the 'double redaction' model appears only in one isolated sentence but unfortunately the idea of two successive redactions itself is not used for locating anger formulae to a specific redactor. The form of the article gives the impression that the idea of double redaction was edited afterwards into the already-existing writing and for this reason the approach was not used in the main part of the analysis.

The concept of God is analysed from various points of view in numerous studies which cannot be listed here and also most theological and exegetical dictionaries or encyclopaedias contain more or less basic information about the anger of God.[40]

Until now there is only one monograph on the present theme: *Anger in the Old Testament* written by B.E. Baloian.[41] The study deals with both human and divine anger in the Old Testament but has its main emphasis on divine anger. Anger expressions are studied throughout the Old Testament, classified into human or divine categories and analysed stressing the following items:

> ...the actual Hebrew terms used, their grammatical status, the synonyms found, the verbs employed with the nouns, the object or subject of the wrath, its motivation, its results, the metaphors used, and the theological themes and intentions which the text possessed... It was only after this

---

40. The following titles are, however, worth mentioning. The articles about God's jealousy by H.A. Brongers, 'Der Eifer des Herrn Zebaoth', *VT* 13 (1963), pp. 269-84; and W. Berg, 'Die Eifersucht Gottes—ein problematischer Zug des alttestamentlichen Gottesbildes?', *BZ* NS 23 (1979), pp. 197-211; the monographs about monistic features in the concept of God by F. Lindström, *God and the Origin of Evil: A Contextual Analysis of Alleged Monistic Evidence in the Old Testament* (ConBOT, 21; Lund: Almqvist & Wiksell, 1983); and about vengeance of God by H.G.L. Peels, *The Vengeance of God: The Meaning of the Root NQM and the Function of the NQM-Texts in the Context of Divine Revelation in the Old Testament* (OTS, 31; Leiden: E.J. Brill, 1994).

41. B.E. Baloian, *Anger in the Old Testament* (American University Studies; Theology and Religion, 99; New York: Peter Lang, 1992).

work had been nearly completed that the work of the other scholars was considered and integrated (p. 5).

Results are presented in the following way. The writer has organized the material into major categories where summaries of the investigation are given and the texts in which it has been difficult to locate any of the created categories are also studied more deeply. At the end of the book there are charts which give basic information about all the anger sayings.

One of the major results is that the motivation of divine anger can be divided into two categories: 'Rebellion' against God or 'the oppression', 'cruelty by one human to another' (Chart 2, pp. 191-210).

Theologically, it has been discovered that justice and love play the dominant role both in the understanding of the function of divine anger and in the appropriateness of human anger. It has also been shown that this understanding was present in many genres of literature: proverbs, historical, narrative, prophetic announcement, hymns, laments, etc. The description of Yahweh's person, as One who contains the passion of anger, does not change ideologically from literary type to literary type (p. 173).

The study raises several methodological questions. Even when the writer does not express his starting point explicitly the approach seems be synchronic, for example, neither the growing process of the text nor the differences between literary units have a special role in the analysis. Even the fundamental and widely agreed results of Old Testament scholarship (e.g. the existence of P material) are ignored in the study. Therefore it is not surprising to find that this position chosen by the author finds its way directly in to the results: 'There appears to be no traditiohistorical development of the theological understanding of anger' (p. 174). The claim that in the theological core of the Old Testament it is not possible to notice any development through the centuries challenges the conventional paradigm so strongly that the claim should be proved with clear and convincing arguments.

Moreover, the whole package of approaches related to the growing process of the text, to the writers and to their socio-historical backgrounds is replaced with the interest in 'Yahweh's person' or in God as 'highly personal and profoundly interested in having relationships with humans' (p. 1). The hidden agenda in Baloian's study seems to be the direct correspondence or even equivalence between the personal and permanent God and the Old Testament texts which reveal this God.

Such an approach raises the expectations of the reader as to how the writer proves these results. On only a few occasions does Baloian's study contain detailed exegesis of the texts and instead of analysis it gives summaries and surveys based on classification and analysis of the texts. Detailed exegesis which takes into consideration the basic results of literary criticism and traditio-historical investigation are ignored as well. The method of study means that the testing of argumentation is usually beyond the reader's ability: thus the reader does not have any tools to make his or her own judgments about the interpretation.

It is hard to avoid the conclusion that the writer's preconceptions of the theme have also strongly affected the categorizing of the material as well as other decisions. The present study will especially challenge Baloian's methodological premises related to the traditio-historical development in the concept of God.

3. *Textual Basis*

In the books of Joshua and Judges the anger of God is characterized through the following words: אף 'nostril, face, anger',[42] כעס (pi./hi.) 'vex, provoke to anger',[43] קצף (qal) 'be wroth',[44] חרה (qal) 'burn, be

42. Used with human beings 42 times and with God 168 times. From the last-mentioned group over 72% are in the following 8 books: Num. (10), Deut. (12), Isa. (20), Jer. (24), Ezek. (11), Ps. (24), Job (11), Lam. (10). See also אנף (qal/htp.) 'be angry', which appears 14 times in the Old Testament: (qal) 1 Kgs 8.46 (= 2 Chron. 6.36), Isa. 12.1; Ps. 2.12; 60.3; 79.5; 85.6; Ezra 9.14; (htp.) Deut. 1.37; 4.21; 9.8, 20; 1 Kgs 11.9; 2 Kgs 17.18. The subject is always God (Ps. 2.12 is the possible exception to this rule).

43. This verb is used 44 times when an individual or a people is the subject and Yahweh is the object: Deut. 4.25; 9.18; 31.29; 32.16, 21; Judg. 2.12; 1 Kgs 14.9, 15; 15.30; 16.2, 7, 13, 26, 33; 21.22; 22.54; 2 Kgs 17.11, 17; 21.6, 15; 22.17; 23.19, 26; Isa. 65.3; Jer. 7.18, 19; 8.19; 11.7; 25.6, 7; 32.29, 30, 32; 44.3, 8; Ezek. 8.17; 16.26; Hos. 12.15; Ps. 78.58; 106.29; 2 Chron. 28.25; 33.6; 34.25; Neh. 3.37. Twice it is a question of human relations (1 Sam. 1.6, 7) and once Yahweh is the subject of the action (Ezek. 32.9). In qal only in Ezek. 16.42 the subject is God; elsewhere it is always a human being (5 times).

44. Appears in the Old Testament 28 times; Yahweh is the subject 17 times: Lev. 10.16; Num. 16.22; Deut. 1.34; 9.19; Josh. 22.18; Isa. 47.6; 54.9; 57.16; 57.17; 64.4; 64.8; Zech. 1.2, 15 (twice); Eccl. 5.5; Lam. 5.22. See also קצף (hi.) 'provoke to wrath', which appears in the Old Testament 5 times (Deut. 9.7, 8, 22; Zech. 8.14;

kindled, of anger',[45] חרון (noun) '(burning of) anger'.[46] In addition, some words which belong semantically rather close to the anger theme and also occur in DtrG, but not in Joshua and Judges, should be mentioned: שנא (qal) 'hate',[47] שנאה (noun) 'hating, hatred',[48] חמה (noun) 'heat, rage, burning anger'[49] and עברה[50] (noun) 'overflow, arrogance, fury'.

4. *The Task*

The history of the investigation with its variety of solutions challenges the present work. The main task relating to the writing process can be focused in the following questions. Is it possible to recognize and to identify redactional activities among those texts that handle the anger of God? If this can be agreed the following question is which model is the most appropriate to describe the growth of the text: double or triple redaction versus an ongoing writing process?

Answers to these questions will open the way for the following level

---

Ps. 106.32), and קצף (noun) 'wrath', which appears in the Old Testament 28 times with this meaning. Only twice is a human being the subject (Eccl. 5.16; Est. 1.18). Usually the subject is Yahweh: Num. 17.11; Deut. 29.27; Isa. 34.2; 54.8; 60.10; Jer. 10.10; 21.5; 32.37; 50.13; Zech. 1.12, 15; 7.12; Ps. 38.2; 102.11; 2 Chron. 19.2; 29.8; 32.26.

45. Yahweh is the subject 41 times: Gen. 18.30, 32; Exod. 4.14; 22.23; 32.10, 11, 22; Num. 11.1, 10, 33; 12.9; 22.22; 25.3; 32.10, 13; Deut. 6.15; 7.4; 11.17; 29.26; 31.17; Josh. 7.1; 23.16; Judg. 2.14, 20; 3.8; 6.39; 10.7; 2 Sam. 6.7; 22.8; 24.1; 2 Kgs 13.3; 23.26; Isa. 5.25; Hos. 8.5; Hab. 3.8; Zech. 10.3; Ps. 18.8; 106.40; Job 42.7; 1 Chron. 13.10; 2 Chron. 25.15.

46. The subject is always God, if Ps. 58.10 is read as *BHS* suggests. The word appears 39 times in Old Testament: Exod. 15.7; 32.12; Num. 25.4: 32.14; Deut. 13.18; Josh. 7.26; 1 Sam. 28.18; 2 Kgs 23.26; Isa. 13.9, 13; Jer. 4.8, 26; 12.13; 25.37, 38; 30.24; 49.37; 51.45; Ezek. 7.12, 14; Hos. 11.9; Jon. 3.9; Nah. 1.6; Zeph. 2.2; 3.8; Ps. 2.5; 69.25; 78.49; 85.4; 88.17; Job 20.23; Lam. 1.12; 4.11; Ezra 10.14; Neh. 13.18; 2 Chron. 28.11, 13; 29.10; 30.8. From the same root is also the form חרי: Exod. 11.8; Deut. 29.23; 1 Sam. 20.34; Isa. 7.4; Lam. 2.3; 2 Chron. 25.10.

47. Deut. 12.31; 16.22; Isa. 1.14; 61.8; Jer. 12.8; 44.4; Hos. 9.15; Amos 5.21; 6.8; Zech. 8.17; Mal. 1.3; 2.16; Ps. 5.6; 11.5; 101.3; Prov. 6.16.

48. In DtrG: Deut. 1.27; 9.28.

49. In DtrG this word appears 5 times with Yahweh as the subject: Deut. 9.19; 29.22, 27; 2 Kgs 22.13, 17.

50. Htp. Deut. 3.26.

of work: dating of the anger theme and identification of its socio-cultural background. In some cases also ideological-criticism can be used.

This study will concentrate in the first part on the exegetical analysis of the texts of Joshua and Judges where the anger of God occurs, whereupon the perspective will be extended in the second part to Deuteronomy, deuteronomistic theology and Priestly Writings in relation to the anger theme.

Chapter 2

ANALYSES OF THE TEXTS IN JOSHUA AND JUDGES

1. *Joshua 23: Other Nations*

At the end of the book of Joshua (ch. 24) attention is paid to the positive outcome of the conquest: Yahweh has brought his people from Egypt, led them through the wilderness into Canaan, driven out the nations and given the Israelites the land. In Joshua 23 this story of conquest is complemented with the threat posed by the existence of remaining nations which would lead the Israelites to be mixed with them and serve their gods. The final outcome of this negative process would mean the destruction of the Israelites, an actualization of the anger of God (23.16).

The basic story (DtrH) in the book of Joshua does not need such a double ending and is, moreover, based on an idea of total conquest of the land. In Josh. 1.1-2 the promise of the land is given without any conditions[1] and its total fulfilment is described in 21.43-45: 'Thus the Lord gave to Israel all the land (כל הארץ).' The theological

---

1. Josh. 1.1-2, 10-11 belong to DtrH and the rest is supplemented through successive additions. 1.3-6 are based on quotes from Deut. 11.24-25 and 31.6-7 (both late) to explicate the promise with a precise description of the areas to possess. The additions end with the *Wiederaufnahme* ('resumptive repetition'); about technique see W.B. Barrick, 'On the Meaning of בית־ה/במות and בתי־הבמות and the Composition of the Kings History', *JBL* 115 (1996), pp. 621-42 (627); repetition of 'to give them'). A different hand, law-oriented writer DtrN, used the same method, *Wiederaufnahme* (repetition of 'be strong and courageous'), to add v. 7 for making the promise of the land conditional. Verses 8-9, which were added also using the *Wiederaufnahme* technique (repetition of 'wherever you go'), already belong to the period of late postexilic Judaism like Pss. 1, 19 (partially) and 119. Late vv. 12-18 already belong to the post-deuteronomistic period. See also the analysis of Josh. 22. Compare Smend, 'Das Gesetz', pp. 494-97 and M. Görg, *Josua* (Die Neue Echter Bibel; Kommentar zum Alten Testament mit der Einheitsübersetzung, 26; Würzburg: Echter Verlag, 1991), p. 11.

programme of the totally fulfilled conquest belongs without any doubt to the core of DtrH.[2] Chapter 24 obviously represents in its basic level this kind of idea; the question about remaining nations is not even mentioned there.

Structural Observations
The above comparison to DtrH texts clarifies the different profile of ch. 23, but there are also some illuminating links between DtrH and ch. 23 that show the method of a successive redactional process; namely, there is a literary connection between Josh. 21.43-45 and Joshua 23, or, to be more precise, there are three quotations in ch. 23 from vv. 21.43-45:[3]

> 21.44aα–23.1aβ
> 21.44b–23.9bα
> 21.45–23.14b.

Thus ch. 23 is based on structuring elements from DtrH, but the writer has changed the focus with the new material surrounding the quotations. He is not only mechanically copying older texts but reinterpreting them, working with the older material but developing it with new ideas. There are, however, no reasons why we should not locate the writer in the same theological stream as DtrH, that is, the deuteronomistic school. Most scholars have identified ch. 23 as one literary unit of the law-oriented deuteronomistic redactor DtrN.[4]

Our next task is to define more closely the structure of the content. The introduction in vv. 1-2a briefly lists persons and draws the scene which is followed by the historical survey in vv. 2b-4. Joshua has allotted the remaining nations—not the *land* as in 24.13—for the Israelite tribes to be driven out of the land. In v. 5 and once more in vv. 9-10 there is an unconditional promise of victory, in both cases followed by exhortation to observe the law of Moses, to love Yahweh and not to join the remaining nations (vv. 6-8 and vv. 11-13). Verse

---

2. M. Noth, *Das Buch Josua* (HAT, 7; Tübingen: J.C.B. Mohr, rev. edn, 1953), p. 133; Smend, 'Das Gesetz', p. 501; Veijola, *Das Königtum*, p. 67; Mayes, *The Story*, p. 44.

3. The close link between chs. 21 and 23 becomes even more obvious if we remember that ch. 22 belongs to the late- or post-deuteronomistic period. See the analysis below on Josh. 22.

4. Smend, 'Das Gesetz', pp. 501-504; Veijola, *Das Königtum*, p. 84; Mayes, *The Story*, pp. 48-51, 56. Against Nelson, *The Double Redaction,* pp. 21, 94-98.

14 confirms the promises, underlining that none of the earlier promises which Yahweh gave to his people had failed. Also this has a negative follow-up in vv. 15-16: 'bad things' will be realized when transgression of the covenant provokes the anger of God and Israelites will 'perish quickly from the good land'.

The chapter is structured in its present shape with alternating promises and warnings:

1. Introduction vv. 1-2a
2. Historical prologue vv. 2b-4
3. Promise v. 5
    4. Conditional promise and warning vv. 6-8
5. Reminder and promise of victory vv. 9-10
    6. New conditional warning vv. 11-13
7. Confirming of the promise v. 14
    8. Confirming of the warning and its argumentation vv. 15-16

Such a structure has some similarities with ancient state treaties which, according to McCarthy, preserved main ideas more or less in the same form through the centuries:

> In spite of variations in different times and places, variations even of some importance, there is a fundamental unity in the treaties. And this unity goes back beyond the Hittite examples into the third millennium. Everywhere the basic elements are the same: the provisions are imposed under oath and placed under the sanction variably made more vivid through the curses which represent (and effect) the dreadful fate of an eventual transgressor. Hence the essential elements of form: stipulations, the god lists or invocations, and the curse formulae which are invariably found in the treaties from Eannatum of Lagash to Ashurbanipal of Assyria.[5]

Neo-Assyrian treaties usually have the following common elements: Preamble, Seal impressions, Divine Witness, Oath/Adjuration, Historical Introduction, Treaty Stipulations, Violation Clause, Traditional Curses, Vow, Ceremonial Curses, Colophon and Date.[6]

---

    5. D.J. McCarthy, *Treaty and Covenant: A Study in Form in the Ancient Oriental Documents and in the Old Testament* (Rome: Pontifical Biblical Institute, new edn completely rewritten, 1978), p. 122.
    6. S. Parpola and K. Watanabe (eds.), *Neo-Assyrian Treaties and Loyalty Oaths* (SAA, 2; Helsinki: Helsinki University Press, 1988), pp. xxxv-xlii. For reviewing the history of research see E.W. Nicholson, *God and his People: Covenant and Theology in the Old Testament* (Oxford: Clarendon Press, 1986), pp. 56-82.

2. Analyses of the Texts in Joshua and Judges

Combinations of blessings and curses is a well-known pattern in the Old Testament. Especially Deuteronomy 28 and Leviticus 26 should be mentioned in this connection, both probably having connections with the covenant structures, although it is not possible to show direct dependence between the Old Testament and specific treaty text. Clearly it would be an exaggeration to claim that Joshua 23 imitates the treaty patterns but, on the other hand, the basic structure of the chapter echoes slightly the most important units of the treaties: historical introduction, treaty stipulations and curses. A major difference to the treaties is the alternating form where promises and warnings follow one after another.[7]

Growing Process of Joshua 23

Literary-critical analysis demonstrates, however, that this structure is a result of a long redactional process. This can be proved by analysing the text carefully. Clear tensions in the content especially, as well as repetitions and other disturbances of the coherence of the text are indicators of redactional activities. The relation of vv. 5a and 9a is very illuminating: both describe how Yahweh fights against other nations, but each text using a different perspective. Verse 5 is a promise of future victories, v. 9a refers to the past tense.

| v. 5a | והוריש אתם מלפניכם | ... | ויהוה אלהיכם |
| v. 9a | מפניכם גוים | | ויורש יהוה |

Verses 6-8 (between these two sentences) stress the importance of observing the written law of Moses (ספר תורת משה)[8] and of not mixing with remaining nations. When we remember that earlier in v. 5 Joshua had promised that there would not be any harm from these nations because Yahweh would drive them out, it is really surprising to concentrate on serious problems caused by the people 'among you'. Actually there is a totally different attitude towards the remaining nations in vv. 1-5 and 6-8. A similar remark can be made about the relation with God: the trust in God's promises is replaced with the strict observation of the written Mosaic law codex, that means, Deuteronomy.

---

7. See also T.C. Butler, *Joshua* (WBC, 7; Waco, TX: Word Books, 1983), p. 253.

8. The expression occurs four times in the Old Testament (all others late): Josh. 8.31; 2 Kgs 14.6; Neh. 8.1.

When a repetition frames the text with divergent content it seems obvious that the writer is using a literary technique called *Wiederaufnahme* (resumptive repetition).[9] Thus vv. 6-9a are a later addition which underlines the conditional character of the promise and also warns Israelites not to have any contact with Canaanites who would lead them to worship Canaanite gods.

The basic text in ch. 23 continues after vv. 1-5 in v. 9b with a somewhat clumsy opening 'and as for you' which binds the plot to the following quote (21.44b > 23.9bα). As in the past 'no one has been able to withstand you', so will it also happen in the future when all enemies will be beaten.

In vv. 11-13 Israelites are warned again in the same spirit as happened earlier in vv. 6-9a, and also in v. 6 and v. 11 there is a similar structure (pf. 2 pl. m. + מאד + ל with infin.). Obviously in vv. 11-13 the same writer as in vv. 6-9a continues the theme 'do not mix yourselves with these nations', but the focus has been changed from a plain warning to the threat to the existence of the nation, 'until you perish from this good land'.

The last quotation from vv. 21.43-45 in v. 14b 'not one thing has failed of all good things' continues the theme of unconditional promises, and seamlessly meshes v. 14 with vv. 1-5, 9b-10. In these verses there is a clear and coherent message about the work of Yahweh in the past and a promise of a good future without any 'buts' and doubts.

The basic text is still supplemented in vv. 15-16 with the last warnings. According to the earlier literary-critical solutions these can be assumed to be a later insertion too. Such a claim is strongly supported with formal observations like the clumsy opening in v. 15 (והיה כאשר) and a repetition from the previous verse.

v. 14   מכל הדברים הטובים אשר דבר יהוה אלהיכם עליכם הכל באו
v. 15   בא עליכם כל הדבר הטוב אשר דבר יהוה אלהיכם אליכם

Also the terminology in vv. 15-16 connects these verses to the secondary text layer of the chapter: soil (אדמה) v. 13, covenant of Yahweh, compare v. 6, serve other gods and bow them v. 7.

In the latter half of v. 16, exactly where the anger theme in ch. 23 becomes obvious, there is a last major question concerning the growing process of the chapter. In the Septuagint v. 16b does not exist,

---

9. See above n. 1.

which can be explained in several ways. Modern commentaries have ignored this information (Noth; Fritz),[10] or have just explained it as a textual error caused by a haplography (Boling)[11] or just given priority to the Hebrew text (Butler).[12] However, according to the Septuagint researchers omissions in the Septuagint text in the book of Joshua may well indicate that the translator did not have those passages in his *Vorlage*, in the Hebrew text he used.[13] The latter understanding can be supported with an observation that in v. 16b the expression 'good soil' (האדמה הטובה) has been replaced with 'good land' (הארץ הטובה), a term earlier in the chapter used only in the basic text and never in the supplementary text layer. The later writer perhaps did not notice the distinction between the words. Even when we cannot be quite sure about the value of Septuagintal evidence its priority can be agreed with minor hesitation. Thus the logical consequence is to locate v. 16b as a late insertion in ch. 23.

As a result of the above analysis the following relative chronology of the growing process can be presented. The basic text contained vv. 23.1-5, 9b-10, which were supplemented with vv. 6-9a, 11-13, 15-16a, and still later by another hand v. 16b.

From Good Promises to the Anger of God
Joshua 23 in its present context offers an extremely good illustration of divergent attitudes towards the land. In the earliest level of the texts (DtrH especially in Josh. 1.2; 21. 43-45; 24*)[14] the land is understood as a free gift of Yahweh. The land is given by Yahweh, and this has already happened during the conquest which led also to the extermination of the enemy (Josh. 11.16-20).

The basic text layer in ch. 23 builds on the ideas of DtrH and even uses earlier text in quotations but also corrects the predecessor's

10. Noth, *Das Buch Josua*; V. Fritz, *Das Buch Josua* (HAT, 7; Tübingen: J.C.B. Mohr, 1994).
11. R.G. Boling, *Joshua: A New Translation with Notes and Commentary* (AB, 6; New York: Doubleday, 1982), p. 521.
12. Butler, *Joshua,* p. 252.
13. Already S. Holmes, *Joshua: The Hebrew and Greek Texts* (Cambridge: Cambridge University Press, 1914), p. 78, gave priority to the Septuagint. Recently also E. Tov, *Textual Criticism of the Hebrew Bible* (Minneapolis: Fortress Press; Assen: Van Gorcum, 1992), p. 228.
14. The asterisk indicates the earliest version of the chapter, which is not, however, explicated.

theological concept with minor relativism. Yahweh 'had given rest to Israel from all their enemies all around' but not total freedom from them and they still exist. Inheritance does not point to the land but to the remaining nations which Yahweh will drive out as he did to other nations earlier. The basic text in Joshua 23 is literarily dependent on 21.43-45 and so it is later than DtrH but earlier than the DtrN-texts, which have been added to it. It is, however, impossible to find any sign of the prophetic editor (DtrP) in the basic layer of Joshua 23.

This optimistic scene is turned upside down in the second text layer in ch. 23. In vv. 6-9a, 11-13, 15-16a a totally different theological attitude controls premises because there is a serious danger that remaining nations will lead Israelites away from Yahweh to worship other gods (עבד אלהים אחרים).[15] To avoid such a development Israelites should 'do all that is written in the book of Moses' (ספר תורת משה),[16] and avoid intermarrying (חתן htp.)[17] with other nations. On the other hand, if Israelites do this and transgress the covenant (עבר ברית)[18] they will be 'destroyed from this good land'. Actually these themes were the fundamental arguments in the article of R. Smend (1971) which led him to reconstruct the nomistic redactional text layer DtrN. Now this identification can be agreed upon but not, however, for the whole chapter as Smend thought—just for the second text layer.

Verse 16b could also belong to the same theological school, although representing a later stage of the process. On the other hand, the possibility of just putting together well-known theological phrases leaves the time span rather open because it was not a complicated

---

15. Cf. Deut. 7.4; 8.19; 13.3, 7, 14; 17.3; 28.14, 36, 64; 29.25; 30.17; 31.20; Josh. 24.2, 16; Judg. 10.13; 1 Sam. 8.8; 26.19; 1 Kgs 9.6; 2 Kgs 17.35. Compare also Jer. 11.10; 13.10; 16.11, 13; 22.9; 25.6; 35.15; 44.3. Mostly DtrN or late dtr. For identifications see Veijola, *Das Königtum,* pp. 57-58.

16. The expression occurs four times in the Old Testament (all others late): Josh. 8.31; 2 Kgs 14.6; Neh. 8.1.

17. In relation to the national activity, otherwise in the Old Testament only in Deut. 7.3 (H.D. Preuss, *Deuteronomium* [EdF, 164; Darmstadt: Wissenschaftliche Buchgesellschaft, 1982], p. 49: very late in Deuteronomy) and Ezra 9.14. In relation to the individual, Gen. 34.9. See also 1 Sam. 18.21, 23, 26, 27; 2 Chron. 18.1. For later development of the issue see Ezra 9.

18. Cf. Deut. 17.2 (Preuss, *Deuteronomium,* p. 54, 136 late dtr); Judg. 2.20 (Smend, 'Das Gesetz', pp. 505-506: DtrN); 2 Kgs 18.12 (Würthwein, *Die Bücher* [1984], p. 410: DtrN).

matter to imitate deuteronomistic language. The absence of the text in the Septuagint refers already to the post-deuteronomistic period.

The discussion above about structural observations leads to the question about the origin of covenant elements. At this moment it is possible to notice that they did not belong to the original shape of the chapter but were introduced through the secondary insertions. Anyhow it might be possible that the existence of covenant patterns affected the writer, perhaps unintentionally. Even when the DtrN-writer is using and applying the language of the Neo-Assyrian or other ancient treaties the aim is to give a theological form of expression to the experience of the people in the frames of political language.

The explicit reference to the exile in the DtrN-layer shows clearly to which period these verses belong. The DtrN-group interpreted the destruction of Jerusalem and the deportation of Judaean people to Babylonia as a sign of God's will and judgment, caused by their forgetting the law of God, joining and intermarrying other nations and serving other gods. Basically all these point to the same question, namely, breaking the first commandment of the Decalogue.

In the latest phase of the textual and theological development of ch. 23, the experience of the exile, losing the good land and perishing was interpreted by the expression that became the paradigm of judgment, namely, the anger of God. It symbolizes the end of the process: total breakdown of the relationship between Yahweh and Israel.

Deuteronomistic theology is not the only context in the Old Testament where the notion of anger is used to describe God. A similar approach is well known also in Lamentations where the exile is interpreted as God's self-revelation and labelled frequently with the expression related to the anger of God (Lam. 1.12; 2.1, 2, 3, 6, 21, 22; 3.1, 43; 4.11; 5.22). Thus the anger of God has been used as a tool of theological self-reflection during and after the exile among the Israelites.

Certain care must be used in interpreting Josh. 23.16b because of its special literary character. But even if it were only an isolated insertion the anger theme represents the crystallization of a long process that has reflected the history and experiences of Israelites during the exile. The anger of God, a well-known concept of the ancient Orient, has absorbed different historical, ideological and theological notions from the period of national crises. This still partly hypothetical result will be illustrated in more detail in the following analysis.

2. *Judges 2: Other Gods*

After the success story in Joshua, which was only slightly overshadowed by some potential threats, Judges 2 turns the view upside down by expressing in practical terms how the Israelites lost every battle because 'the hand of the Lord was against them to bring misfortune'. The essential part of the plot is the anger of God which was provoked by the Israelites (vv. 12, 14, 20). Chapter 2 has traditionally had a strong position in the interpretation of the book of Judges for it works like an introduction or programme for the following stories.

The original literary context for Judges 2 was the end of the book of Joshua (24.28) from where the plot continued in vv. 2.7-10—in other words, this is part of the story created by DtrH.[19] As in the earlier text of DtrH (Josh. 21.43-45; 24*), Israel is a witness for 'the great work' of Yahweh. The beginning of the new era is related to the change of the generation because those who grew up after their ancestors 'did not know the Lord or the work that he had done for Israel'.

It has been obvious to the scholars during this century that vv. 11-23 are deeply deuteronomistic, but until now a satisfactory agreement about the growing process of the text has not been achieved. A loose frame for most of the proposals has been an idea about the basic text (DtrH) supplemented with later dtr-insertions.[20]

Growing Process of the Text

Indicators of the incoherent nature of the text are observable throughout the passage: abandoning Yahweh and worshipping Baal is mentioned twice in vv. 11-13 as well as the raising of the judges in vv. 16, 18. In a similar way the opponents of Israel are called 'plunderers' in vv. 14a, 16a and 'enemies' in vv. 14b, 18a. These double expressions do not bring any additional information into the text but are more likely to be signs of the literary working process.

---

19. Cf. Smend, 'Das Gesetz', p. 506; Mayes, *The Story*, pp. 59-60; M.Z. Brettler, 'Jud 1,1-2,10: From Appendix to Prologue', *ZAW* 101 (1989), pp. 433-35; Becker, *Richterzeit*, p. 68.

20. Smend, 'Das Gesetz', pp. 504-505; H. Spieckermann, *Juda unter Assur in der Sargonidenzeit* (FRLANT, 129; Göttingen: Vandenhoeck & Ruprecht, 1982), pp. 209-10 n. 116; Mayes, *The Story*, p. 76.

2. Analyses of the Texts in Joshua and Judges

Among the thorny problems in ch. 2 the question about the role of the judges seems to be the best item to start with. Since the turn of the century scholars have agreed that v. 17 is a later insertion.[21] Using the modern literary-critical paradigm we can notice how the writer applies the *Wiederaufnahme* (resumptive repetition) technique. In the following figure, insertions are indented and the literary loans expressed with arrows.

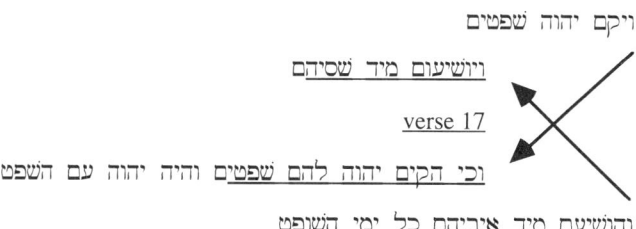

The function of the insertion is obvious when the role of the judges in v. 17 is compared with the framing verses. Verses 16a and 18aβb give the role of warrior or hero to judges, but v. 17 supposes that judges were somehow related with the law and commandments of Yahweh and they prevented people from following other gods. There is no doubt about the writer who made the insertion in vv. 16b-18aα: DtrN. In a similar way there is no reason to deny the assumption that the framing verses which describe the judges as political persons would not belong to DtrH.

Verses 19-23 make the supplemented theme even more evident. Because the Israelites have broken the covenant, followed other gods and bowed down to them the anger of Yahweh was kindled against Israel, and as a final punishment Yahweh cancelled his promise to drive out the remaining nations before the Israelites. Also here the hand of DtrN can easily be recognized.

On the basis of its different style, theological viewpoint and grammatical form, v. 22 is generally classified as a late and secondary insertion,[22] probably no longer belonging to the deuteronomistic school.

---

21. Kuenen, *Historisch-kritische Einleitung* (1.2), p. 9; K. Budde, *Die Bücher Richter und Samuel: Ihre Quellen und ihr Aufbau* (Giessen: Ricker, 1890), p. 92; Nowack, *Richter*, p. 19; W. Richter, *Die Bearbeitung des 'Retterbuches' in der deuteronomischen Epoche* (BBB, 21; Bonn: Hanstein, 1964), p. 33; Smend, 'Das Gesetz', p. 505; Mayes, *The Story*, p. 67.

22. Richter, *Die Bearbeitung*, p. 37; Smend, 'Das Gesetz', p. 505; Mayes, *The Story*, p. 68; Becker, *Richterzeit*, p. 101.

A second observation concerns the alternation between the terms 'plunderers' and 'enemies', which are both used twice in parallel sentences in v. 14. Even if it might be difficult to be precise about the difference it seems to be the best solution to interpret 'enemies' as foreign attackers from abroad, while 'plunderers' can be foreigners but still living in the same country.[23] Thus it is possible to connect the term 'enemies' with the idea of a totally fulfilled conquest (DtrH uses 'enemies' in Josh. 21.44), and the term 'plunderers' with the ongoing battle with the nations among the Israelites. The latter idea occurs in the texts belonging to DtrN. According to this solution and earlier analysis v. 14b is a landmark for DtrH and v. 14a comes from the pen of DtrN.

Third, in the content and vocabulary of vv. 11b-13 there is a close correspondence with vv. 16b-18aα, 19-21, 23 (follow other gods, bow down to them, worship the Baals/gods, abandon Yahweh/turn aside from the way), which is a clear indicator of belonging to the same theological circle, DtrN. Within vv. 11b-13 there is, however, the last literary-critical item that can be classified as a disturbance to the coherence of the text: the worship of Baal and abandoning of Yahweh, repeated in *chiastic* order.

vv. 11b-12aα	ויעזבו את יהוה	ויעבדו את הבעלים
v. 13	ויעבדו לבעל ולעשתרות	ויעזבו את יהוה

The probable explanation for this phenomenon is the *Wiederaufnahme* used for adding v. 12aβb into the text. The function becomes obvious when we notice that the insertion is a quotation from Deut. 6.14 which emphasizes the loyalty and obedience to Yahweh and forbids idolatry (quotations underlined).

Deut. 6.12-15	Judg. 2.12
השמר לך פן תשכח את יהוה	ויעזבו את יהוה אלהי אבותם
אשר הוציאך מארץ מצרים	המוציא אותם מארץ מצרים
מבית עבדים את יהוה אלהיך תירא	
ואתו תעבד ובשמו תשבע	
לא תלכון אחרי אלהים אחרים	וילכו אחרי אלהים אחרים
מאלהי העמים אשר סביבותיכם	מאלהי העמים אשר סביבותיהם
	וישתחוו להם ויכעסו את יהוה
כי אל קנא יהוה אלהיך בקרבך	
פן יחרה אף יהוה אלהיך בך	Cf. v. 2.14
והשמידך מעל פני האדמה	

---

23. Becker, *Richterzeit*, pp. 75-76.

The description of the reverse events in v. 12 explicates the reasons and gives detailed grounds for the anger of Yahweh which led to national catastrophe and loss of full autonomy. The quotation from Deuteronomy, just a couple of passages after the Decalogue, also verifies the accusation of breaking the covenant in v. 20.

After literary-critical analysis of the text it is possible to reconstruct the following formation process. The basic text (2.7-11a, 14b-16a [not the gloss in v. 15aβ] and 18aβb) which develops the ideas from Josh. 21.43-45; 24* comes from the pen of DtrH. A large additional literary layer belongs to the later deuteronomistic circle DtrN which contains at least *two different strata* because there is a nomistic insertion inside the DtrN text. Verses 2.11b-14a, 16b-18aα, 19-21, 23 belong to the DtrN-circle. Finally, vv. 2.15aβ, 22 are isolated insertions or glosses.[24]

Other Gods versus the Anger of Yahweh
Literary growth from the basic text of DtrH to the DtrN-layers reflects also the motives for the theological reinterpretation process. A primary concern of DtrH is to describe national history from the viewpoint of the relationship between Yahweh and the people. Even when the earliest text layer does not use the common deuteronomistic vocabulary and might be called thin or weak in theological articulation it is only an optical illusion.

Actually DtrH has a clear and distinctive theological plot but it is hidden or expressed implicitly through the historical plot. In vv. 2.7-11a, 14b-16a and 18aβb, DtrH launches a new paradigm for the national salvation history and shows that old creeds do not have any meaning in the present moment if they are not actualized in Israel's life. Every new generation has to face the reality that all the good things that Yahweh had given them can be lost. Whenever the knowledge about 'Yahweh or the work that he had done for Israel' disappears among the Israelites Yahweh will actively 'bring misfortune', but also in a day of oppression 'be moved to pity' and save

---

24. Cf. the result of Becker, *Richterzeit*, pp. 68-72, 74-82, 99-106. To DtrH belong vv. 2.8-12aα (mistakenly [?] in p. 82 v. 12aβb also to DtrH), 14b-16a, 18a (from word ויהי), b and to DtrN belong vv. 12aβb, 13-14a, 16b-18aα*, 19-21. Verses 22-23 are a still later insertion.

his nation without any condition or requirements. In other words, the experience of the Exodus generation is put in a nutshell.

Although DtrH shows that the Israelites are completely dependent on Yahweh and that the historical crises are caused by the Israelites' lack of memory about the real basis of their existence, he does not even mention idolatry or God's anger. These elements do not appear until the texts of the DtrN-group.

The rather low theological profile in the first text layer opened the way for later supplements to reflect the historical plot in explicit theological terms. The severe state of the nation exists also in the DtrN circle but attention is paid to the reasons for 'the great distress', or to be more precise, the exile. Even when the word 'exile' is not mentioned in Judges 2 it is obviously the historical context from which the argumentation grows. Additionally, explicit references to the exile appear in the DtrN texts in Joshua 23.

The theology of anger rises from the soil of the exile and from the hard experiences of the Israelite people. The DtrN circle strives, however, to give theological grounds for the national disaster, pointing out that the final reason lies in the bad behaviour of Israel, that is, abandoning Yahweh and worshipping other gods provoked (ויכעסו את יהוה) Yahweh's anger to kindle (ויחר אף יהוה) against Israel.

Thus the anger theology of DtrN sounds strongly relational: anger is Yahweh's reaction towards Israel's choice to abandon Yahweh and turn to other gods. Such a constellation is reminiscent of the marital case of adultery, where the husband's reaction is described with the word *jealousy* (קנא/קנאה), a term also used in deuteronomistic texts (e.g. Deut. 4.24; 5.9; 6.15; Josh. 24.19). Using similar ideas DtrN makes Yahweh react like a betrayed oriental husband because Israel has broken the relationship. Another metaphor close to the previous one comes from oriental vassal treaties. As in Joshua 23 the term 'covenant' (v. 20 ברית) appears here also in a context that speaks of Israel's disloyalty to Yahweh, to his commandments and to his 'voice'. In v. 20 the reason for kindling the anger of Yahweh is related to breaking the covenant and disobedience to its stipulations.

Beyond this deeply affective and anthropomorphic language lies the profound theological core: according to the deuteronomistic concept the identity of Israelite religion is compressed into the form of the first commandment in the Decalogue. In deuteronomistic theology it has the central position for defining the essence of faith. Yahweh, who

2. Analyses of the Texts in Joshua and Judges

had brought Israel from Egypt and given the land to Israel, required absolute devotion without any exceptions.

It is not surprising to notice that such hardline ideologies blossom during the extremely difficult period when the existence of the nation as well as the meaning of traditional beliefs and creeds was threatened. However, the logic of deuteronomistic theology, especially DtrN, is impossible to understand fully without recognizing its fundamental motive: the idea that God is the ultimate guarantor for the realization of justice. This concept was connected with the difficult experiences of Israel during the exile by using the anger of God as a link with other ideas.

Deuteronomistic anger theology is like a junction of three roads: experiences of life, belief in justice happening on earth[25] and a monotheistic concept about God as final actor in the nations' history. According to this logic the exile was explained as the result of Israel's transgressions. Because they had not worshipped only Yahweh but other gods as well—obviously a historical fact—Yahweh punished them by using Babylonia as a whip.

Anyhow the last word in the sermon of the deuteronomistic theologians was not about punishment but about national salvation through dogmatic reformation based on strict monotheistic faith without any room for other gods or goddesses. Showing the reasons for past misfortune, deuteronomistic theologians pointed the new way to a future still overshadowed by the threat of the anger of God.

3. *Judges 3.7-11; 10.6-16: Other Gods 2*

The theological programme in Judges 2 written by DtrH and largely supplemented by the DtrN-circle has two relevant parallels in Judg. 3.7-11 and 10.6-16. Both passages also mention the anger of God (3.8; 10.7).

Generally the story in 3.7-11 is understood to be built on material

---

25. Before and during the exile fulfilment of justice as well as punishment following the transgressions were basically understood collectively when the fate of the nation was explained. Only after the exile was there a turn to more individualistic direction. G. von Rad, *Theologie des Alten Testaments*. I. *Die Theologie der geschichtlichen Überlieferungen Israels* (Munich: Chr. Kaiser Verlag, 8th edn, 1982), pp. 382-408; S. Japhet, *The Ideology of the Book of Chronicles and its Place in Biblical Thought* (BEATAJ, 9; New York: Peter Lang, 1989), pp. 156-65.

which does not have a historical basis. The otherwise unknown king Cushan-rishathaim is first localized in Mesopotamia (ארם נהרים) but later in the same passage in Aram (ארם). The uncertain identity of the king and the location have their counterpart in the Israelite saviour Otniel, son of Kenaz, who is probably a literary loan from similar contexts in Josh. 15.17 and Judg. 1.13. Otherwise the passage contains nothing but deuteronomistic phraseology. Soggin expresses agreement among scholars in the following way:

> In any case, one firm point is the fact that it is not possible to find any kind of basis in history that we can recognise or that can appear probable.[26]

Most scholars identify 3.7-11 to the first dtr-redactor.[27] Verses 10.6-16 were earlier seen more or less as an elohistic story with some deuteronomistic colouring[28] but more recently it has been accepted to be a wholly deuteronomistic creation.[29]

Structure and Terminology
Synoptical examination of Judg. 2.11-19, 3.7-11 and 10.6-16 demonstrates unambiguously that they are related to each other through common vocabulary, dtr-phraseology and—even more importantly—common structure. The following tables show the similarities.

---

26. J.A. Soggin, *Judges: A Commentary* (OTL; London: SCM Press, 1981), p. 47. In a similar way also among others, Nowack, *Richter*, p. 23; C.F. Burney, *The Book of Judges: With Introduction and Notes* (London: Rivingtons, 2nd edn, 1920), p. 64; Noth, *Überlieferungsgeschichtliche Studien*, pp. 50-51; Mayes, *The Story*, p. 73; Becker, *Richterzeit*, p. 106.

27. Nowack, *Richter*, p. 23; Burney, *The Book of Judges*, p. 64; Noth, *Überlieferungsgeschichtliche Studien*, p. 50; Smend, 'Das Gesetz', p. 116. Cf. also Mayes, *The Story*, pp. 71-72.

28. B. Stade, 'Zur Entstehungsgeschichte des vordeuteronomistischen Richterbuches', *ZAW* 1 (1881), pp. 339-43 (342); Nowack, *Richter*, p. 97; Burney, *The Book of Judges*, pp. 293-295.

29. Wellhausen, *Die Composition*, p. 214; Noth, *Überlieferungsgeschichtliche*, p. 53; J.P. Floss, *Jahwe dienen—Göttern dienen: Terminologische, literarische und semantische Untersuchung einer theologischen Aussage zum Gottesverhältnis im Alten Testament* (BBB, 45; Bonn: Hanstein, 1975), p. 385; Veijola, *Das Königtum*, p. 46; Smend, 'Das Gesetz', p. 116; Spieckermann, *Juda*, p. 210; Mayes, *The Story*, p. 76.

2. Analyses of the Texts in Joshua and Judges

Phraseology in Judg. 2.11-19		3.7-11	10.6-16
v. 11 (DtrH)	ויעשו בני ישראל את הרע בעיני יהוה	v. 7	v. 6
v. 12/v. 13 (DtrN)	ויעזבו את יהוה	cf. v. 7[30]	v. 6, 10, 13
v. 13 (DtrN)	ויעבדו לבעל ולעשתרות	v. 7	v. 6,10
v. 14 (DtrN)	ויחר אף יהוה בישראל	v. 8	v. 7
v. 14 (DtrN)	ויתנם ביד	cf. v. 10	–
v. 14 (DtrH)	וימכרם ביד	v. 8	v. 7
v. 16 (DtrH)/v. 18 (DtrN)	ויקם יהוה	v. 9	–
v. 16 (DtrN)/v. 18 (DtrH)	ויושיעום	v. 9	cf. vv. 12-14

The Structure of Judg. 2.11-19	3.7-11	10.6-16
1. Disobedience of Israel v. 11 (DtrH)	v. 7	v. 6
2. Abandon Yahweh v. 12/13 (DtrN)	v. 7	v. 6
3. Worshipping other gods v. 11/13 (DtrN)	v. 7	v. 6
4. Anger of Yahweh v. 12/14 (DtrN)	v. 8	v. 7
5. Punishment v. 14-15 (DtrH/N)	v. 8	v. 7-9
6. Delivery v. 16/18 (DtrH/N)	v. 9-10	(v. 16/ch. 11)[31]

Observing the structure uncovers the connection between the passages but besides that it shows how the stories in chs. 3 and 10 are evidently built on the material coming from the pens of both DtrH and DtrN in ch. 2. Without the supplements added by DtrN there would not be such common ground; the parts written by DtrH are used as well. Such a far-reaching similarity is impossible to understand without common authorship. As Judg. 2.11-19 was largely rewritten by the DtrN redactors, one would presumably find the solution in both Judg. 3.7-11 and 10.6-16 from a similar direction. However, it must be remembered that later redactors can also use known expressions, thereby imitating their predecessors.

From Mercy to Conditional Delivery

In vv. 3.7-11 typical DtrN-expressions concentrate in vv. 3.7aβ-8aα (underlined part) in a way that demands attention.

ויעשו בני ישראל את הרע בעיני יהוה וישכחו את יהוה
אלהיהם ויעבדו את הבעלים ואת האשרות ויחר אף יהוה

---

30. In v. 3.7 the verb is שכח (in v. 2.11 עזב).

31. Cf. also the shorter structure given by F. García López, 'Analyse littéraire de Deutéronome, V–XI', *RB* 84 (1977), pp. 481-522 (513): (1) Sin of Israel, (2) Anger of Yahweh and (3) the punishment. This structure is common also in other dtr-texts, e.g. Deut. 6.14-15; 7.4; 8.19-20; 11.16-17; 1 Kgs 11.9-11; 14.9-10.

בְּיִשְׂרָאֵל וימכרם ביד כושן רשעתים מלך ארם נהרים ויעבדו
בני ישראל את כושן רשעתים שמנה שנים

There is no doubt that vv. 3.7aβ-8aα belong to the DtrN writer but the rest of the passage fits perfectly with the theology and plot of DtrH. This solution is practically based on analysis of ch. 2 because in ch. 3 there are no literary-critical criteria, though evidence of vocabulary is present.[32]

Relation of the passages in chs. 2 and 3 are like a programme and practical model. Everything expressed in ch. 2 in theoretical terms had its counterpart in ch. 3. This is true whether we follow the first or the second text layer, the latter of course building on the former and supplementing it. The reason for creating such a story in vv. 3.7-11 was that it offered an excellent possibility of illustrating theological principles which the writers wanted to stress.

The theology of DtrH grows directly from the source material that describes the judges as political leaders, and smoothly creates larger writing based on the older traditions that were describing national heroes as actors used by Yahweh. Transition to the later phase of the same school brings remarkable theological changes into the basic paradigm of the text, but also creates an incongruity between the tradition material and the DtrN-theology.

Supplementing the stories in chs. 2 and 3 with the themes of worship of other gods, breaking of the covenant and the anger of Yahweh, created an imbalance between these chapters and the following stories. After ch. 3 in the book of Judges, polemic against the breaking of the first commandment of the Decalogue nearly disappears, but vv. 10.6-16 form an exception to this rule: the question about other gods is once more the key issue, as in chs. 2–3.

The growth of the passage Judg. 10.6-16 has been explained by using the same pattern as in chs. 2–3: the basic text belongs to DtrH but it is supplemented by DtrN.[33] Even if this hypothesis is taken into

---

32. Veijola, *Das Königtum*, p. 46 (DtrH: 6aα, 7b*, 8a*, 8b*; the rest DtrN); Becker, *Richterzeit*, pp. 104-106 (DtrN: 3.7aβ-8aα; the rest of DtrH).

33. Veijola, *Das Königtum*, p. 46 (DtrH: 10.6aα, 7b*, 8a*, b*; the rest of DtrN); in a similar way also Spieckermann, *Juda*, p. 210 n. 117; Mayes, *The Story*, p. 69 (Dtr[1] 10.6aα, 7-9; Dtr[2] 10.6aβb, 10-16); Becker, *Richterzeit*, pp. 210-12 (DtrH: 10.6aα (until to the word הבעלים), 7bα[1]β, 8a, 9b, 10a; DtrN: 10.6aβb (from ואת העשתרות), 7a, bα[2] (only ביד פלשתים), 8b, 9a, 10aβ (from לאמר) -16.

consideration as one possible solution it still contains some unanswered difficulties. The major argument against this approach is the context of vv. 6-16. The preceding verses briefly mention two judges, Tola and Jair, ending with the death and burial of the latter. Correspondingly v. 17 continues the plot describing how the Ammonites started to plan military action against the Israelites. Verses 6-16 have, however, already reacted to this question in a strange way. First, the whole episode is motivated by the breaking of the first commandment of the Decalogue, and second, some military operations are mentioned in vv. 7-9. Finally, the amazing thing is the discussion between the Israelites and Yahweh which ends with some kind of implicit promise of help or at least compassion from God, which in other connections indicated the raising of the deliverer. After all this in vv. 17-18 the whole plot goes back to square one without reflecting in any way the previous occurrence of conflict with the Ammonites.

Thus it does not seem reasonable to try to uncover a shorter DtrH layer in vv. 6-16 *if* it contains the attack of the Ammonites (in vv. 8-9). Actually the plot runs fluently from vv. 3-5 to vv. 17-18, which shows that those passages are not just isolated pieces of tradition but already a formation made for the book of Judges. The question of commanders of Gilead[34] about the new leader connects the death of Jair in v. 5 to the acute threat on the Ammonites' side. Despite the fact that quite often DtrH opens stories with a theological introduction, that is, about the phrase evil-doing, this should not taken for granted, because at the beginning of the Abimelech story the phrase does not occur.[35]

The second alternative to solve the tension could be just to take the opening phrase in v. 10.6aα, 'The Israelites again did what was evil in the sight of the Lord', and v. 7b*, 'and he sold them into the hand of the Ammonites'. Even in this shortest possible introduction a minor structural weakness still exists because vv. 10.6aα and 7b* fit better with the struggle in vv. 8-9 than with vv. 17-18.

Comparison between these two options is rather difficult because both solve the basic incongruity of the text but neither of them can be proved to be right. With some caution priority can be given to the

---

34. The word 'people' (העם) seems to be a later insertion, perhaps added by DtrN. So Veijola, *Das Königtum*, p. 47 n. 59.

35. That may have caused the later insertion to be added in vv. 8.33-35 in criticism of idolatry.

first solution to identify vv. 6-16 as a later insertion stressing the criteria of better logic and fluency of the text.

Material collected from sources can be found in vv. 10.1-5 and 11.1-40*, while the redactional plaster of DtrH is in vv. 17-18,[36] and finally the major insertion supplemented by DtrN is in vv. 10.6-16.

The theological shift from the tradition material through the DtrH to DtrN has been dramatic. While DtrH agrees with the theological stress found from the source material, the same cannot be said about the theology of DtrN. From that point of view smaller pieces of tradition concerning Tola and Jair as well as the larger story about Jephthah did not articulate theological dimensions sufficiently and were dogmatically misleading because the major question relating to the first commandment was totally ignored. This pressure caused DtrN to write a new introduction to the Jephthah episode, which should be interpreted as an illustration of a theological programme using the historical frames and form, that is, writing a sermon in a narrative way. Parallel to this method is the later insertion made in Judg. 6.7-10 where the unknown prophet explains the historical disaster with the help of a similar theological paradigm. The secondary literary character of the latter case is confirmed by 4QJudg^a which omits vv. 6.7-10 and very probably represents an earlier phase of the literary growth.[37]

Supplementing the text with the passages 3.7aβ-8aα and 10.6-16 DtrN powerfully reformed the concept of God in those chapters by introducing the anger theme and making God's promises to the Israelites conditional. While DtrH did not make any conditions for Yahweh's mercy and help (see especially v. 2.18b) the same cannot be said about the theology of the DtrN group. People had to move their idols away, confess their sins and cry for help before Yahweh reacted. These were stipulations for the Israelites which they should have fulfilled to receive the liberation or delivery from the hands of the evildoers, but instead of that they had abandoned Yahweh and worshipped other gods.

---

36. Verse 17b can be a later insertion added by DtrN. So Veijola, *Das Königtum*, p. 47 n. 59.

37. Ulrich E. *et al.* (eds.), *Qumran Cave 4, IX Deuteronomy, Joshua, Judges, Kings* (DJD, 14; Oxford: Clarendon Press, 1995), p. 162; J. Trebolle Barrera, 'Textual Variants in 4QJudg^a and the Textual and Editorial History of the Book of Judges', *RevQ* 54 (1989), pp. 229-45 (238, 245).

As in previously examined chapters here also the worship of other gods is connected to the anger of Yahweh and to the national crises. The theological paradigm produced by the DtrN-group follows the model: the Israelites abandon Yahweh and worship other gods and therefore Yahweh brings a large-scale disaster to confront them, which finally leads to their repentance and delivery.

If we take into consideration also the results of the previous analysis we can see the same model from a different point of view; namely, DtrN writings are dated to the exilic period which means that the writers themselves were living in the middle of national crises and needed an explanation for themselves and their contemporaries. The destruction of Jerusalem and the deportation of the upper class to Babylonia were facts that demanded a new theological orientation. If Yahweh was still understood to be the ruler of historical processes he would have to be responsible for the disaster. The solution for this was found in the notion of anger caused by idolatry. Thus the actual responsibility for all evil was not Yahweh but Israel itself. Projecting their own case back into the ancient stories of the nation's early period, the writers were giving sermons to their contemporaries. With these passages DtrN writers wanted to demonstrate people's responsibility for the national crisis and use that to promote their new theological programme.[38]

All the features of this school stress the absolute and distinctive nature of their faith: obey and worship only Yahweh, do not have any connections to other nations or their gods or otherwise the anger of Yahweh will kindle and he will lead the whole nation to face trouble. DtrN writers introduced the idea of the anger of Yahweh as one of the major key issues to the deuteronomistic ideology when they identified the political and historical experiences of exile with the anger of Yahweh. Simultaneously they also created an extremely powerful theological logic to persuade the Israelites to change their understanding about God towards an exclusive monotheism.

4. *Joshua 7: Fire and Stones*

Passages analysed until now have all been following very stereotyped

---

38. Cf. M. Smith, *Palestinian Parties and Politics that Shaped the Old Testament* (New York: Columbia University Press, 1971), pp. 44-45, 50-53 ('an apologetic theodicy').

patterns to describe the theology of anger, always giving the same context: abandoning Yahweh and worshipping other gods. Joshua 7 opens a new path because these questions are not even mentioned here. However, in this case also the Israelites are confronting a national defeat in a war. The misfortune of the Israelites in ch. 7 is sandwiched between glorious victory in Jericho in ch. 6 and the slaughter of Ai in ch. 8.

Growth of the Text
Former examinations have proved that the Achan episode is not one literary unit but a combination of different elements. The traditio-critical approach tried to explain the differences with an idea about two accounts coming from different sources secondarily connected to each other, namely, stories about Ai and Achan.[39] In some sense this can still be agreed but present theories about the gradual growth of the text during a long successive writing process offer a more precise way to describe the relation of the two literary units.

Most probably the oldest layer which belongs to DtrH can be found in vv. 2-5 and then the follow-up in ch. 8, that is, the Ai story which also carries the general plot in the book of Joshua. The rest of ch. 7 (vv. 1, 6-26) certainly comes from a different kind of background and is most likely inserted secondarily into the text.[40] The task of this study is to identify and date more precisely this section which also includes the sayings about the anger of Yahweh.

Theological Context of the Achan Episode
T. Veijola has collected a convincing list of arguments which point out that the Achan story is deeply connected with late deuteronomistic theology—especially the prayer in vv. 7-9 has its counterparts in exilic repentance theology—but also the theme of conquest, battle against other nations and name theology has deuteronomistic roots.[41]

39. Noth, *Das Buch Josua*, p. 43.
40. T. Veijola, 'Das Klagegebet in Literatur und Leben der Exilsgeneration am Beispiel einiger Prosatexte', in J.A. Emerton (ed.), *Congress Volume: Salamanca 1983* (VTSup, 36; Leiden: E.J. Brill, 1985), pp. 286-307 (299-305). According to Veijola, a major part of the addition belongs to DtrN but vv. 11aβb, 12b, 13b, 21-23 and parts of v. 24aα could be dated to the post-deuteronomistic period; B. Peckham, *The Composition of the Deuteronomistic History* (HSM, 35; Missoula, MT: Scholars Press, 1985), p. 34, thinks that the whole Josh. 7 is written by redactor dtr2.
41. Veijola, 'Das Klagegebet', pp. 299-305.

2. Analyses of the Texts in Joshua and Judges 49

Obviously this creates the earliest possible date but not the latest because the theological language as well as the deuteronomistic ideas were flourishing through the centuries. Moreover, the decisive question is whether the story was influenced by the later theological streams represented in chronistic and priestly writings.

The following arguments try to illustrate that besides the deuteronomistic theology vv. 1, 6-26 contain a lot of material that belongs to the later postexilic period. The story begins with the phrase 'But the Israelites broke faith in regard to the devoted things' (וימעלו בני ישראל מעל). Similar expression appears *only* in the P-tradition and in late postexilic writings.[42] Another sign of the P-style is the structural idea of the story: sanctification (קדש in v. 13). This very common verb in P is never found elsewhere in DtrG in a similar context.[43] The third typical P-expression is (יהודה) למטה 'tribe (of Judah)'.[44] The fourth linguistic feature in the same direction can be found in v. 19: the word תודה appears in the Old Testament 15 times, mostly in the psalms. In DtrG there is a single appearance. In most of the Old Testament passages the meaning of תודה is 'thanksgiving, praise'. In 7.19 the meaning is, however, more like 'confession'; a similar use of the verb can be found only once in the Old Testament and that is in the chronistic environment, in Ezra 10.11.[45]

Also the basic concept חרם, 'devoted or banned thing', seems to be used in a special way. The traditional deuteronomistic usage for the term was to destroy or ban something: Deut. 13.17-18; 20.17-18, a town with its people; Deut. 7.26, a statue of an idol; 1 Samuel 15,

---

42. In total 35 times from which 6 belong clearly to P (Lev. 5.15, 21; 26.40; Num. 5.6, 12, 27). To the similar tradition circle belong passages in Ezek. 14.13; 15.8; 17.20; 18.24; 20.27; 39.23, 26. There are 15 chronistic appearances: 1 Chron. 2.7; 5.25; 10.13; 2 Chron. 12.2; 26.16, 18; 28.19, 22; 29.6; 30.7; 36.14; Ezra 10.2, 10; Neh. 1.8; 13.2). Cf. also Dan. 9.7 and Prov. 16.10 (dating?). The last two passages in Deut. 32.5 and Josh. 22.16, 20, 31 are dependent on P-tradition.

43. In the Old Testament more than 70 times, mostly P. In DtrG 1 Sam. 7.1; 1 Kgs 8.64 (E. Würthwein, *Die Bücher der Könige: 1. Kön. 1–16* [ATD, 11.1; Göttingen: Vandenhoeck & Ruprecht, rev. edn, 1985], p. 101: postdtr); 2 Kgs 10.20 (Y. Minokami, *Die Revolution des Jehu* [GTA, 38; Göttingen: Vandenhoeck & Ruprecht, 1989], pp. 101-107: from the fourth century).

44. With the meaning 'tribe' 183 times in the Old Testament, almost just in P. In DtrG only in Joshua (7.1, 18; 13.15, 24; 15.1, 21; 17.1; 18.21; 19.1, 24, 40— BDB, p. 641: all P).

45. BDB, p. 392.

enemies and their animals. In the priestly tradition similar terms are used to describe things devoted to God and belonging to the sphere of the holy where only sacral persons can be in touch with these things: Lev. 27.21, 28, fields or other owned items, Num. 18.14; Ezek. 44.29, whatever is devoted to God. In the Achan story the חרם concept is partly something which should be banned and destroyed in the battle of Jericho, but on the other hand, items stolen by Achan seem to belong to Yahweh, that is, to the sacral world. These two different traditions are somehow connected and even assimilated in Joshua 6–7.

Finally, the closest larger parallel passage to Joshua 7 is in the chronistic milieu: Ezra 10.1-17. Also on that occasion have the people been unfaithful (vv. 2, 10 מעל) and they have repented before God to turn the anger of God away (v. 14 חרון אף). Furthermore, the property of unfaithful people has to be destroyed, that is, devoted to God (חרם). In prayers too there are some similar features to Ezra 9.1-15, 10.2-4 and Joshua 7. Diversities between the stories in Joshua 7 and Ezra 10 indicate that the passages are not literarily dependent upon each other but more probably are reflecting similar theological backgrounds. Apart from these arguments from ch. 7 it has already been widely recognized that vv. 6.18-19, which prepare the soil for the Achan story, belong to the priestly and/or chronistic literary environment.[46]

The combination of different theological streams in Josh. 7.1, 6-26 makes the passage difficult to classify. Deuteronomistic and/or exilic questions are clearly visible in the chapter but also signs of postexilic theology are present. Thus we may locate v. 1, 6-26* in the open terrain somewhere between deuteronomistic, priestly and chronistic traditions. For the purposes of dating this means at the end of the sixth or beginning of the fifth century BCE.

Some smaller parts of the text which do not exist in the Septuagint probably come from a still later pen with a meaning intended to intensify the cultic features of the story. This is especially true in v. 6 where the word 'ark' ארון appears in the Hebrew text but not in the Septuagint.

Theological Emphasis: God of Fire and Stones
In Joshua 7 we may notice different kinds of theological stresses. If

---

46. Veijola, 'Das Klagegebet', p. 303 n. 64, interpreting all priestly and chronistic elements as secondary additions; Schwienhorst, *Die Eroberung*, pp. 113-35.

we just read the basic text of DtrH (7.2-5; 8.1 onwards) we have a story speaking about battle, defeat and victory with the help of God. This level says nothing about disobedience, the anger of God, law or judgment but focuses on the Israelites' total dependency on the help of Yahweh during the conquest.

The large addition in vv. 1, 6-26 used these frames for illustrating a different kind of theological message. Joshua 7 has been formerly described as 'a piece of narrative theology',[47] which indicates that the focus of the Achan episode lies not upon historical information but upon its ideological level. As a result of the analysis the whole secondary layer was dated to the transition period between deuteronomistic and priestly/chronistic theology. A similar shift can also be noticed in the theological emphasis reflecting the shift from the deuteronomistic period, which is concretely discernible in the growing stress laid on one's individual responsibility and on the more extreme demand to obey the law. God does not turn from his anger until Achan is removed from among the Israelites and stoned, that is, the transgression and punishment of one person has become the dominant question and requirement for the well-being of the whole community.

When these ideas are examined, remembering the theological backgrounds of DtrH and DtrN especially, the difference is remarkable. DtrH did not give any demands for God's work but showed how God freely reacts when the Israelites are in a hopeless situation. In the writings of DtrN national defeats are explored at a collective level for rationalizing the exile and reforming religious practices, especially those relating to the first commandment. All this indicates changes in the concept of God when we come from early exilic time (DtrH) to the early postexilic era as well as leaving the deuteronomistic school to enter the sphere of the priestly/chronistic world.

Every analysed deuteronomistic (DtrN) text related to the anger of God has used the following paradigm: Israelites worshipped other gods—the anger of Yahweh kindled—Israelites abandoned other gods and served Yahweh for receiving delivery/victory, and so on. In the Achan story the pattern is different: (חרם) the transgression of one person—the anger of Yahweh kindled—stoning and burning of the

---

47. Veijola, 'Das Klagegebet', p. 304. See also R. Polzin, *Moses and the Deuteronomist: A Literary Study of the Deuteronomic History*, I (New York: Seabury, 1980), p. 114.

guilty with his family and all 'contaminated belongings'. Worth noticing is the fact that in the Achan story the external threat caused by other nations with their gods has turned to the internal question of the community about strict demands of how to worship Yahweh in an appropriate way.

Always essential for theology are the individuals and their communities beyond the texts: why did the community need this kind of image about God? What can we say about the community, about the soil where this theology has its roots? Or does the story reflect the opinion of extremists, a party of fundamentalists, inside the community?

The text was dated to the early Persian period when the temple was rebuilt and rededicated. When the closer historical setting is searched, one option would be to link the present story with the issues related to the temple or the rising demands of (priestly?) circles who wanted to make a clear distinction between sacral and profane. Even when we cannot illustrate a coherent and clear picture about that period it seems obvious that the temple community or the priestly circle needed various new laws as well as practical guidelines.

Moreover, it is possible that the different religious groups or sects may have represented various opinions and attitudes towards the temple and items belonging to it and this could have motivated somebody to illustrate the issue through a narrative sermon projected into the ancient period. The only certain thing about the sects of this period is that there existed various groups and that at the present moment we cannot identify them without falling easily into the pit of circular arguments between the texts and the social world behind them.[48]

Anyhow it seems obvious that the leaders of the community who were able to produce or delegate somebody else to write texts were worried about how to control the development of the process. Through the Achan story they could stress serious and strict demands

---

48. A clear and well-argued synthesis of different hypotheses concerning the sectarianism is collected by L. Grabbe, *Judaism from Cyrus to Hadrian* (London: SCM Press, 1992), pp. 103-12. See also R. Albertz, *A History of Israelite Religion in the Old Testament Period* (2 vols.; OTL; trans. J. Bowden; Louisville, KY: Westminster/John Knox Press, 1994), II, pp. 464-93, who has created an inspiring combination about the dynamics of the postexilic power relations and religious groups.

to obey Yahweh even in details related particularly to the temple.

One interesting remark should still be added. After locating the story within the early postexilic period the next step is to identify Achan somehow in the sociological strata of society. What group of the society does he represent or which group would identify themselves with Achan?

Achan is described with the following characteristics. He belongs to the Israelites and takes part in the fight, neither as a war hero nor as coward, he belongs to the tribe of Judah, to the clan of the Zerahites, to the family of Zabdi and is the son of Carmi. His energy and intelligence can also be mentioned, making possible his stealing of spoils during the war. Achan is not labelled as strange, corrupted or evil but as a person who cannot resist temptation. In a larger frame he also represents the generation of pioneers who were willing to fight for their land and living space. To sum up: Achan seems to be decent and energetic but a rather average person among his contemporaries—actually, his main characteristic is that he is one of us, or anybody could be Achan.

It is also possible that this kind of text may have been produced to legitimate the punishment of individual members who belonged to the community. Compared to the earlier texts analysed above, the transgression of the story is insignificant, not abandoning God but taking spoil, a normal habit in war. One of the main motives beyond the text could be the need for greater devotion, purity and perfection in the community, or a need to make everybody in the community follow the extremely strict rules of the leaders. The early postexilic period probably contained a lot of dreams about the perfect future as well as the disappointments of everyday life—the latter part of the book of Isaiah (chs. 40–55 versus chs. 56–66) confirms the tension.

The Achan story is clear evidence of rising fundamentalism during the postexilic period. The essence of fundamentalism was to keep individuals under strict control requiring adherence to the ideals of the leaders (or extremists among the leaders) which demanded absolute truth and purity in ethnic questions (Josh. 23; Ezra 9–10), dogmatic issues (Deut. 13) or in respect of the sacral (Josh. 7). Common to all these strivings is that they try to protect the community and its faith in an ideal form but that they simultaneously take that fatal step over the border of intolerance and inhumanity.[49]

---

49. T. Veijola, 'Wahrheit und Intoleranz nach Deuteronomium 13', *ZTK* 92

54   *God, Anger and Ideology*

The existing threat of excommunication and even stoning in the name of God gave an extremely powerful weapon to those exercising power in the temple community. The God of anger, stones and fire did not leave much space for individual opinions or negotiations: the law of God had to be obeyed in the form expressed and interpreted by the leaders. The contemporary concept of God, especially the idea about the anger of God, seems to mirror the power relations of the community and to illustrate especially the inner dynamics of the society.

5. *Joshua 22: God between the Parties*

The theme of the anger of God is transposed to an entirely new setting in Joshua 22 where the threat of anger is caused by building an altar for Yahweh, that is, worshipping him. As in Joshua 7 in the Achan story, we are dealing here with internal questions of Yahweh's religion without any relation to the external danger. The transition of context is also reflected in the terminology: the expression used in passages analysed earlier, 'the anger of God kindles' (חרה אף יהוה) has changed to 'be angry, be wrathful' (v. 18 קצף) and 'wrath appears' (v. 20 היה קצף). In addition to the new terms, the anger has lost its subject and become anonymous divine power.

The central issue from which the anger theme grows in Joshua 22, is the relation between the Israelites in Canaan and two-and-a-half tribes on the other side of Jordan, especially the arrangements related to the cult.

Prelude: Sharing Welfare with the Kindred (Joshua 22.1-8)
Verses 1-8 describe the leadership of Joshua[50] and vv. 9-34 that of Phinehas. Joshua is not even mentioned in the latter part of the chapter: he just totally disappears from the screen and his position is replaced by a *priest*. According to the large consensus among scholars

---

(1995), pp. 287-314 (310-14), evaluates the extreme positions taken in Deut. 13 positively as a struggle for authentic and absolute faith. If the texts are read like an insider this conclusion may be taken but then the intention of the research to enable a fair dialogue between the religious parties beyond the texts is endangered.

    50. The words 'servant of Yahweh' עבד יהוה do not exist in the LXX. When the same phenomenon occurs in Josh. 1.1 and 1.15 it is more likely that those words were not in the *Vorlage* of the LXX translator and are later additions to the Hebrew text (Tov, *Textual*, p. 328).

2. Analyses of the Texts in Joshua and Judges

the literary disunity of Joshua 22 is obvious. Verses 9-34 are generally understood to be a later supplement to vv. 1-8 and linked somehow with the P-tradition.[51]

In addition to these already firm results one can find different layers in vv. 1-8. In vv. 2-3 Joshua declares that two-and-a-half tribes have fulfilled their obligations and could return to their home district, which also happens in v. 6. Between the exhortation to go and its realization we can find a 'new' additional demand to observe God's commandments very carefully (רק שמרו מאד לעשׂות את המצוה ואת התורה). On the other hand, the question of observing the law is never mentioned in the context of tribes east of the Jordan (Num. 32; Deut 3.12-20; Josh. 1.12-18). Probably v. 5 is a later pious reinterpretation of vv. 1-4.[52] The small comment in v. 7a is a typical interpolation explaining the area which belonged to the tribe of Manasseh.[53]

Also vv. 7b-8 are a later addition to vv. 1-4, 6 because people had already been sent home and blessed in v. 6, but Joshua repeats the sending in v. 7b.[54] This time the tribes get new orders 'to divide the spoil of your enemies with your kindred' (or 'with brothers' עם אחיכם). Also the clumsy beginning in 7b (וגם כי) and repeated words indicate disturbances in the coherence of the text. The writer has used *Wiederaufnahme* in the following way:

v. 6   ויברכם יהושע וישלחם וילכו אל אהליהם
v. 7b   וגם כי שלחם יהושע אל אהליהם ויברכם

Thus in vv. 1-8 we can find four different layers: the basic text in vv. 1-4 and 6, and three different additions to it in vv. 5, 7a and 7b-8. The fifth layer in ch. 22 is is found in vv. 9-34 which requires at least the existence of vv. 1-4, 6; 7b-8.

---

51. Kuenen, *Historisch-kritische Einleitung* (1.1), p. 103 (later than P); Wellhausen, *Die Composition*, p. 133; Noth, *Das Buch Josua*, p. 133; Smend, *Die Entstehung*, p. 114 (added by final redactor of Pentateuch); Mayes, *The Story*, p. 160; Becker, *Richterzeit*, pp. 68-69; Fritz, *Das Buch Josua*, pp. 220-22.

52. C. Steuernagel, *Das Deuteronomium: Das Buch Josua* (HKAT, 1.3; Göttingen: Vandenhoeck & Ruprecht, 1900), p. 236; Smend, 'Das Gesetz', p. 501 n. 29.

53. Kuenen, *Historisch-kritische Einleitung* (1.1), p. 131; Wellhausen, *Die Composition*, p. 133. Verse 7a differs from its context also with the use of word 'tribe': v. 1 מטה—v. 7a שבט.

54. Kuenen, *Historisch-kritische Einleitung* (1.1), p. 131; Wellhausen, *Die Composition*, p. 133; J.S. Kloppenborg, 'Joshua 22: The Priestly Editing of an Ancient Tradition', *Bib* 62 (1981), pp. 347-71 (352).

Taking issue with the vast majority of investigations of vv. 1-4 and 6 cannot be attributed to the deuteronomistic writer of the basic text (i.e. to DtrH) because of the strong connection to the post-deuteronomistic passage Josh. 1.12-18[55] which points to the later time. Linguistic evidence supports this attribution, for the central concept in vv. 1-4 and 6 is 'the land of the possession' (ארץ אחזה) which appears in the Old Testament only in the tradition circle of P and never in the dtr context.[56] Also the word מטה in a meaning 'tribe' is typical of the P-texts.[57] Similar post-deuteronomistic or P connection is obvious in the expression 'to keep the charge [of Yahweh]' (שמר את משמרת).[58]

The earliest level in ch. 22 (vv. 1-4, 6) concentrates on the legitimization of the position of two-and-a-half tribes east of the Jordan after the conquest, that is, confirming a genuine Israelite status and linkage to the cult community. In clear words the verses stress that if someone lives outside Palestine it does not mean giving up their connection to Israelite society.

Reading this text in the postexilic situation in which the verses were written, the message becomes even more meaningful. In that context two-and-a-half tribes can also be understood as representatives of those Israelites who were living outside Palestine, perhaps no longer in captivity but in Diaspora. Their status is confirmed because they

---

55. Josh. 1 has grown in a very long literary process in which vv. 1.1-2, 10-1,1 represent the earliest stratum (DtrH). It is supplemented with quotations from Deuteronomy in vv. 1.3-6, and still later by DtrN in v. 7. Verses 8-9 belong to the phase of 'Torah piety'. Verses 1.12-18 were added during the post-deuteronomistic period.

56. In the Old Testament this expression appears only eight times. After Josh. 22.4, 9, 19 it can be found only in Pentateuchal P-passages: Gen. 36.43 (secondary to P?; M. Noth, *Überlieferungsgeschichte des Pentateuch* [Stuttgart: W. Kohlhammer, 1948], p. 18 n. 52: secondary addition to P or to the whole Pentateuch); Lev. 14.34; 25.24; Num. 35.28. The word אחזה is used only in P-traditions (P, H, Ezek.) and in chronistic texts.

57. Meaning 'tribe', 183 times in the Old Testament, almost only in P. In DtrG only in Joshua (7.1, 18; 13.15, 24; 15.1, 21; 17.1; 18.21; 19.1, 24, 40—BDB, p. 641: all P.

58. Mostly this expression appears in contexts related to cultic duties in P or the corresponding stream of tradition (Num. 3.7, 28, 32, 38; 8.26, 35; 18.3, 4, 5; Ezek. 44.8, 15, 16; 48.11; Zech. 3.7; Neh. 12.45; 1 Chron. 23.32). More generally about the keeping of the law also in Gen. 26.5 (secondary to Yahwist?); Lev. 18.30; 22.9; Num. 9.19, 23; Deut. 11.1; Josh. 22.3; 1 Kgs 2.3. Cf. also Mal. 3.14.

2. *Analyses of the Texts in Joshua and Judges* 57

have carried out their part in history for the well-being of the Israelite community.

An interesting nuance of this relationship is added in the secondary text layer in vv. 7b-8 stressing the great 'wealth' which the two-and-a-half tribes possess as spoil: 'very much livestock, silver, gold, bronze, and iron, and a great quantity of clothing'. Wealth achieved through the battles is not meant just for their own good but also to be shared with the kindred or 'brothers'. It is very hard to find any sense to these verses if they are interpreted as an element of conquest story where all the men have naturally taken part in the fight and would share the spoil with their families.

However, if the postexilic social context is kept in mind, it is rather easy to find the point of the text. The life in the Diaspora had already settled down during two to three generations—at least the people had gained a remarkable position in the economic sphere and had wealth; 'much livestock, silver, gold, bronze and iron'.[59] Because the growing riches are never divided equally, especially in unbalanced political situations, it is probable that some parts of the Jewish community were certainly suffering from lack of wealth while others succeeded in collecting substantial possessions. Beyond this rather obvious basic setting full-scale exploration of the details are not possible. Perhaps the exhortation was addressed to the wealthier part of the Diaspora community to help their fellow countrymen. It is also possible to think about the distinction between the rich in the Diaspora and the poor in Palestine. The latter interpretation is supported by the fact that 'the kindred/the brothers' in similar literary connections always referred to the tribes living in Palestine and never to the wives and children left on the other side of the Jordan (Num. 32; Deut. 3.18-20; Josh. 1.12-18; 22.1-5). In a similar way centuries later New Testament writings exhorted Hellenistic Christians to help poor 'brothers' living in Jerusalem (Gal. 2.10; Acts 11.29).

The Anger of God and the Postexilic Power Struggle
Verses 9-34 continue the same theme, but focus on the question of the religious freedom of non-Palestinian Israelites to practise their faith by building an altar to Yahweh. Unlike the first part of the chapter the latter do not legitimate the national status of tribes east of the Jordan but deny certain religious activities to them.

59. Albertz, *A History*, II, pp. 370-74.

On their way to the other side of the Jordan, two-and-a-half tribes 'built there an altar by the Jordan, an altar of great size' which caused a bitter conflict, being the reason for the *'war'* between the tribes and other Israelites led by the priest Phinehas. In the name of the whole cult-community Phinehas and representatives of the tribal families accuse the tribes east of the Jordan of *'rebellion against Yahweh'*. Rebellion would cause divine anger directed to the whole Israelite cult community (אל כל עדת ישראל). The decisive point in the confrontation is whether the altar is only a 'witness' (עד) of the eastern tribes belonging to the Palestine-centred Yahweh religion, or if it is a real altar, that is, a symbol of the freedom to practise the Yahweh-religion and also perform offerings.

Attempts to reconstruct the historical events beyond the present story, or even the core of it coming from the latter part of the second millennium BCE, will be unsuccessful, as the present form written in a style reminiscent of P totally hides all earlier stages—if these existed at all.[60] On several occasions the perspective of the plot is in the future, like speaking about the fate of children in vv. 24-28, which strengthens the assumption that the writer is most likely thinking about contemporary issues of the latter part of the fifth century BCE, but projecting the case into the conquest period.

The major religious basis for the writer is the centralization of the cult (Deut. 12), an issue that no longer needs to be argued but requires application to the new circumstances. Without the existence of the deuteronomic or deuteronomistic centralization laws as a given or as an inherited element of writer's ideology, the strict demands in vv. 9-34 would not have been understandable.

In any case the issue about the Yahweh-altar outside Jerusalem was such a burning theme in the fifth century that it needed this kind of illustration. From the writer's point of view (and that of other people represented) even the possibility that somebody is going to build a new Yahweh-altar generates the threat to the contemporary religious system.

Is it possible to find any historical connection related to the issue? Although the historical information is rather sporadic some proposals can be given. One possibility could be the Samaritan schism which led to the founding of the independent community and building the temple

---

60. Different hypotheses are described by Kloppenborg, 'Joshua 22', pp. 347-49, 370-71.

2. Analyses of the Texts in Joshua and Judges 59

on Mount Gerizim. However, the first textual evidence of the temple appears late, in 2 Macc. 6.2, which leaves the earlier development open. Also the temple in Leontopolis built by Onias IV (or III) in the latter part of 160s BCE (Josephus, *Ant*. 12.9; 13.3)[61] is out of the question because of its late dating.

In contrast, the temple of the Jewish colony on Elephantine Island should be taken into consideration in this connection. The community of Elephantine, which had its historic roots in the sixth century, followed Egyptian laws and ways of living.[62] Their religious background was in Yahweh religion but not in a form represented in exilic and postexilic mainline streams, that is, deuteronomistic and P-texts. With Yahweh (or Yaho יהו) also the Anat-Yaho (ענתיהו) was worshipped, probably as a spouse of the former.[63] Yahweh is mentioned also in connection to Anat-Bethel (ענתביתאל) and Eshem-Bethel (אשמביתאל), additional evidence of non-monotheistic religious practices reflecting earlier pre-exilic reality in Palestine.[64]

One of the most important Elephantine documents in this connection is the letter[65] from the year 407 which was addressed to Bagohi, Persian governor in Judah. The letter describes the destruction of the Yahweh temple (in 410) and requests help for the repair of the temple to resume the cult, including meal offering, incense and burnt

---

61. B. Porten, *Archives from Elephantine: The Life of an Ancient Jewish Military Colony* (Berkeley: University of California Press, 1968), p. 118; Grabbe, *Judaism*, pp. 266-67.

62. A. Cowley, *Aramaic Papyri of the Fifth Century* (Oxford: Clarendon Press, 1923), p. xvi; E.G. Kraeling, *The Brooklyn Museum Aramaic Papyri: New Documents of Fifth Century B.C. from the Jewish Colony at Elephantine* (London: Oxford University Press, 1953), pp. 42-44; Porten, *Archives*, p. 20.

63. Cowley, *Aramaic*, pp. 147-48 (no. 44.3).

64. Cowley, *Aramaic*, p. xix; F. Stolz, 'Monotheismus in Israel', in O. Keel (ed.), *Monotheismus im Alten Israel und seiner Umwelt* (Biblische Beiträge, 14; Freiburg: Katholisches Bibelwerk, 1980), pp. 143-84 (172-74); H. Vorländer, 'Der Monotheismus Israels als Antwort auf die Krise des Exils', in Bernard Lang (ed.), *Der einzige Gott: Die Geburt des biblischen Monotheismus (*Munich: Kösel Verlag, 1981), pp. 84-114 (102).

65. Two copies of that letter were found in Elephantine (both are copies or drafts from the original). Cowley, *Aramaic*, pp. 108-22 (nos. 30 and 31), dates the letters to the year 408; B. Porten and A. Yardeni, *Textbook of Aramaic Documents from Ancient Egypt. I. Letters* (Jerusalem: Hebrew University, 1986), pp. 68-75 (A4.7 and A4.8), on the other hand, date them to 25.11.407 (20th of Marḥesvan, year 17 of King David).

offerings (מנחה ולבונה ועלוה; A4.7.21). The reference to the similar (?) letter (A4.7.18-19) sent to the leaders of the Jerusalem cult-community, naming the high priest Johanan (יהוחנן) and his brother Ostanes (אוסתן), shows that they must have known the situation but ignored it.

The tension, or even break, between the two Jewish groups probably grows from their different religious ideologies, the Elephantine group representing more reforming or tolerating trends and Jerusalem leaders representing more a strictly exclusive monotheistic interpretation. If the information about purifying the Jewish community, especially priests, from mixed marriages (Ezra 9–10) reflects more generally the governing trends in Jerusalem in the latter part of the fifth century, such a confrontation is more than to be expected. Besides the polytheistic features in their faith, the Elephantine community had close relations with other ethnic minorities on the island.[66]

Despite the ignorance of the Jewish leaders the Persian governor reacted positively to the rebuilding of the temple, mentioning also the offerings (A4.9; Cowley no. 32). After mentioning the meal offerings and the incense one would expect a word about the burnt offerings but that is missing in the letter, which can be interpreted as a denial of larger cultic activities or as a political statement against animal sacrifices. Also the interference of Jerusalem Jewish leaders is not out of the question.

Elephantine correspondence ends soon after this and the following history of the rebuilding plans of the temple is unknown, but the Jewish community at Elephantine was probably destroyed in a decade. There are, however, signs of the Jewish settlements in Egypt during the following centuries as well as temples. Finally, a positive attitude towards a temple in Egypt is reflected in Isa. 19.18-22, which illustrates the diversity of Jerusalemite opinions towards the temples in Egypt.[67]

The destruction and rebuilding plans of the temple on Elephantine are dated to the same period as the writing of Josh. 22.9-34. We

---

66. U. Winter, *Frau und Göttin: Exegetische und ikonographische Studien zum weiblichen Gottesbild im Alten Israel und in dessen Umwelt* (OBO, 53; Göttingen: Vandenhoeck & Ruprecht, 1983), p. 505.

67. Kraeling, *The Brooklyn*, pp. 117-19; O. Kaiser, *Das Buch des Propheten Jesaja: Kapitel 13–39* (ATD, 18; Göttingen: Vandenhoeck & Ruprecht, 3rd rev. edn, 1983), pp. 86-89.

2. Analyses of the Texts in Joshua and Judges

know also that the leaders of Jerusalem were aware of the Elephantine situation because the community sent a request for help to them. Is it possible to read the answer of the Jerusalemite priests in Josh. 22.9-34? An affirmative answer would place too large a burden on the shoulders of the present analysis, but to some extent we can agree. We may assume that the leaders of the Jerusalem cult community opposed the repair plan of the syncretistic Yahweh temple. Further, the dating of the text seems to be based on rather realistic analysis and very probably there is a congruence between the opinions of the Jerusalem leaders and the story in Josh. 22.9-34. Thus, the logical conclusion is that the Elephantine case may be reflected somehow in Josh. 22.9-34.[68]

It might not be an accident that in 22.11 the temple is built near the Jordan *river* and later in the story the land of the eastern tribes is defined to be *unclean* (טמאה). Especially the last-mentioned item fits better with Egypt than with the land given by Yahweh to his people as an inheritance.

There is also a larger structural changing process inside Judaism which is related to the present topic, namely, the origin and growth of the synagogue institution among the Jewish population in the Diaspora which can be also dated about to the same period.[69] From this point of view Joshua 22 can also be related to the broader disintegration process that challenged the cult centralization laws. Practically, synagogues were substituted for the temple cult, and as a new element in the religious system they also needed adjustment and regulations.[70]

Both the Elephantine community and the origin of the synagogue institution are representative of the disintegration trends within Judaism during the postexilic period which, in many aspects, is still unknown. This situation leaves so many uncharted areas on the map that special caution is needed when connecting the text with one of the rare, known historical processes. However, especially the Elephantine case works quite well also as an illustration of the text and as parallel historical material concerning the social world of the writers.

---

68. See also J.G. Vink, 'The Date and Origin of the Priestly Code in the Old Testament', *OTS* 15 (1969), pp. 1-144 (48-50, 76).
69. G. Stemberger, *Das klassische Judentum: Kultur und Geschichte der rabbinischen Zeit 70 n. Chr.—1040 n. Chr.* (Munich: C.H. Beck, 1979), pp. 92-96.
70. A. Menes, 'Tempel und Synagoge', *ZAW* NS 9 (1932), pp. 278-76 (270-72).

What is the function of the anger of God in Joshua 22, interpreted in the light of the fifth century sociopolitical background? The writer is aware of earlier ways of using the anger of God in the early postexilic period, referring directly to the Achan story in v. 20 but using the terminology coming from P-traditions. The expression 'the anger of Yahweh kindled against' (. . . ב יהוה אף ויחר) is replaced by the anonymous divine anger that just appears against 'the congregation of Israel' without a clearly defined subject (קצף היה ישראל עדת כל על).

Just as Achan was a warning showing what would happen if someone rebelled against God, likewise the eastern tribes could trigger a corresponding catastrophe. From the writer's point of view all those strivings which challenge the Jerusalem-centred cult system can cause divine anger. Thus the threat of the anger rises not from the soil of idolatry or other questions related to the first commandment, the theme so important for deuteronomistic writers, but from the internal issues of Yahweh religion. According to the dtr-theology the main issue *was to serve the right God*, Yahweh, but the P-circle focuses on *the right way of serving God*. The priestly theology of anger differs radically from the deuteronomistic viewpoint which concentrated on the struggle against idolatry. In a new historical situation burning questions are related to the cultic obedience inside the Yahweh religion.

Ideologically the independent Yahweh-altar outside Jerusalem would have meant giving up the absolute power of Jerusalem leaders over the sacrificial cult. Offerings belonged to the core of Jewish religion in which the temple was the place to meet Yahweh. In the cult centralization (Deut. 12) offerings elsewhere in Palestine were prohibited but the new historical context in the Diaspora created a new dilemma.

Obviously there had been a tremendous pressure for organizing the cult in the Diaspora but all these ideas are strongly controlled in Joshua 22 which is like a new regulation for adjusting the older law. The altar as a symbol of participation for the cult community was acceptable while the fear of the altar generated extremely strong expressions like 'war', 'rebellion' and (divine) 'anger'. These negative statements in story form show the limits of the ideological tolerance of Jerusalem priests who connected the political terminology (war, rebellion) with the theological discussion between Jewish groups about the proper way of organizing the cult. According to the story only a right deed in a wrong place legitimates making war against other Jewish groups (v. 12).

The message of the story is that the divine authority is the symbol of the ultimate limit which nobody can cross without endangering the existence of the whole cult community. In an illuminating way the authority of God and the authority of Jerusalem priests are assimilated in v. 19: 'Do not rebel against the Lord, or *rebel against us*.' In practice this means that the anger of God has become an instrument of ideological debate for legitimating the unity of the community as well as the Jerusalem-centred leadership of the Yahweh-cult.[71]

The anonymity of divine anger as well as the assimilation of the authority of God and the authority of the leaders creates an ideological cover which prevents plain argumentation and shifts the theological debate beyond the limits of communication. In Priestly theology the sovereignty and transcendence are characteristic features in the concept of God[72] which are here transposed also to the sphere of social interaction and ideological confrontation.

In a similar way to the P-theology's use of divine authority and anger to cover the real power game, the knowledge about Elephantine correspondence can balance the situation, give more detailed information about other viewpoints, or even perhaps give a voice to the silent opponents of P-theologians. Only on very rare occasions is it possible to form a picture where the opinions and arguments of non-biblical writers are represented, instead of being labelled as sectarians or heretics. If the conclusions of the present analysis are correct the combination created from Elephantine correspondence and Joshua 22 can offer an illustrative picture about the dynamics of the Jewish groups. In that process the anger of God has been used in a context where the theological concept is interwoven with the fabric of social, cultural and historical questions as well as with the realities of ideological and political decision making. The postexilic power struggle also gave an opportunity for Jewish authorities to use the anger of God as a superior defence for their theological interpretations.

---

71. Görg, *Josua*, p. 102. For the similar trends in other P-texts see Kloppenborg, 'Joshua 22', p. 359.

72. Already C. Steuernagel, *Lehrbuch der Einleitung in das Alte Testament* (Tübingen: J.C.B. Mohr, 1912), pp. 229-30: 'Dieser [Gottesbegriff] ist stark transzendent; eine tiefe Kluft besteht zwischen Jahve einerseits und den Menschen und überhaupt der Welt andererseits.'

The Bible has a dominant role in theological discussion about divine revelation, or even as the only real source for searching for God. If this preoccupation is followed it leads one also to accept the darker side in the concept of God. As an example of this:

> The conclusion to be drawn from this section is that instead of being an element foreign to God's nature, vengeance is an essential component of the Old Testament revelation of God. The vengeance of God is an extension of his holiness and zeal, it is paired with his wrath and it stands in service of his righteousness.[73]

For avoidance of too-narrow theological statements, ideological criticism should be used, not as the only or main methodological perspective, but as a supplement of an already-rich range of approaches.[74]

In Joshua 22 ideological criticism reminds us that in theological discussion the Bible should not only be understood as the revelation by God or about God but also as a battlefield of human interests where God is used as a tool by different ideological groups.

6. *Joshua 9: Divine Order*

Compared to all the other texts analysed until now this chapter reveals a strange net of cunning (v. 4), lies (vv. 9-13) and unexpected connections between Israelites and other ethnic groups (vv. 22-27)—in the middle of the conquest story. Finally, when all plots and lies are uncovered there is only one obstacle that prevents the Israelites from exterminating Gibeonites according to the principles of the warfare laws: an oath given by the leaders of the congregations protects Gibeonites because it cannot be broken without the danger of divine 'wrath' which would 'come upon' the congregation (v. 20 ולא יהיה עלינו קצף).

Joshua 9 and 22 are connected to each other by common anger expressions as well as the anonymity of divine anger. In Joshua 22 the question is how the cult community organizes its relation to other Israelite groups. However, in ch. 9 the problem concentrates on the close relation between the Israelites and the people in Gibeon.

---

73. Peels, *The Vengeance*, p. 292.
74. A good introduction to ideological criticism is written by David J.A. Clines, *Interested Parties: The Ideology of Writers and Readers of the Hebrew Bible* (JSOTSup, 205; Sheffield: Sheffield Academic Press, 1995), pp. 9-25.

2. Analyses of the Texts in Joshua and Judges

Growing Process of the Text
In order to locate the anger theme within the chapter as well as to analyse it against the background of its historical and social connections we first have to allow space for literary-critical analysis.

A profound literary tension in the chapter is the competition for the leading role in the story between Joshua and the leaders of the congregation (נשיאי העדה). Additionally, sometimes 'Israelites' (בני ישראל) are the subjects of the activities. It is very illuminating for the story that in a crucial moment, when the final decisions are made concerning the Israelites' acts towards the Gibeonites, Joshua is not even mentioned (vv. 18-21)—as happened in ch. 22. On the other hand, the leaders of the congregations are mentioned for the first time only in v. 15.[75]

Probably vv. 18-21 are a later insertion, confirmed by the divergence of the vocabulary employed in other parts of the story. 'Leaders of the congregation' (נשיאי העדה) and 'whole congregation' (כל העדה) are non-typical expressions in deuteronomistic theology but occur frequently in Priestly circles.[76] The anger expression (לא) היה קצף על points in the same direction. In the Pentateuch it occurs only twice and both belong to P: Num. 1.53 and 18.5.[77] Besides vv. 18-21, vv. 15b and 14 also share a similar background.[78]

---

75. Noth, *Das Buch Josua*, pp. 55-57, 59, thinks that Joshua was incorporated secondarily into the story and the original text was speaking about Israelites and their leaders which were later reformulated in the Priestly tradition into the leaders *of the congregation*. This very hypothetical solution seems to lead the analysis into a dead end.

76. נשיאי העדה Exod. 16.22; Num. 4.32; 16.2; 31.13; 32.2; Josh. 22.30 (for the last see pp. 54-64 above; for other identifications see Smend, *Die Entstehung*, p. 48; and M. Noth, *Das vierte Buch Mose: Numeri* [ATD, 7; Göttingen: Vandenhoeck & Ruprecht, 1966], pp. 109, 205). Cf. also Exod. 34.31; 35.27, Josh. 17.4; 22.14, 32. Moreover, the word for 'cult community, congregation' (העדה) is a typical P-term while deuteronomistic writings use the word קהל.

77. See Smend, *Die Entstehung*, p. 48. Cf. also Josh. 22.20; 2 Kgs 3.27 (an enigmatic text); 2 Chron. 19.10; 24.18; 32.25.

78. Corresponding solutions are represented also by Steuernagel, *Lehrbuch*, p. 277 (supplement to P-tradition in fourth century); Kuenen, *Historisch-kritische Einleitung* (1.1), p. 100 (second P redactor); J. Halbe, 'Gibeon und Israel: Art, Veranlassung und Ort der Deutung ihres Verhältnisses in Jos. IX', *VT* 25 (1975), pp. 613-41 (613-16); A.D.H. Mayes, 'Deuteronomy 29, Joshua 9, and the Place of the Gibeonites in Israel', in N. Lohfink (ed.), *Deuteronomium: Entstehung, Gestalt und Botschaft* (BETL, 68; Leuven: Leuven University Press, 1985), pp. 321-25

The second major disturbance in the coherence of the text lies in vv. 6-8 where the roles of Joshua and the 'Israelites' are interwoven. In v. 6b there is also a double introduction (ויאמרו אליו ואל איש ישראל) after which Joshua disappears from the scene in vv. 6b-7 which is strange because it was Joshua whom the Gibeonites were looking for (v. 6a). Very probably there is a secondary insertion which is added with the *Wiederaufnahme*.

    v. 6b ויאמרו אליו
    v. 8b ויאמרו אל יהושע

Thus the insertion starts in v. 6b (from ואל איש) and ends in 8aα (to the words ויאמרו אל יהושע). In a similar way also vv. 11bα²β, 15aβ and 16aβ, which add the covenant theme into the peace-making act, belong to the same layer.

As a conclusion from the literary-critical analysis, ch. 9 can be seen as a result of three successive writers from which the *first* described the peace which Joshua made with the Gibeonites in vv. 9.3-6a (until ויאמרו אליו), 8aβ (from עבדיך אנחנו) to 11bα¹ (until אליהם), 12-13, 15aα, 16aα, 16b-17a (except ביום השלישי), 22-23 (except וחטבי עצים ושאבי מים), 24-26.[79] *The second* writer supplemented the story with the covenant theme in vv. 9.6b (from ואל איש)–8aα (until אל יהושע), 11bα²β, 15aβ, 16aβ. The *third* literary layer is in vv. 9.14, 15b, 18-21.[80]

Partners against the Laws of Warfare
The story plot in the basic literary layer is based on the existence of the laws of warfare in Deut. 20.10-18 as well as their application in Joshua 6 (Jericho) and 7–8 (Ai).[81] According to them all enemies living nearby should be killed.

---

(325). Görg, *Josua,* p. 42 (post-dtr). Against M. Ottosson, *Josuaboken: En programskrift för davidisk restauration* (Acta Universitatis Upsaliensis; Studia Biblica Upsaliensia, 1; Uppsala: Uppsala Universitet, 1991), p. 83, who rejects the literary-critical method as too simple.

 79. Halbe, 'Gibeon', pp. 620-25, 640-41, finds the core in vv. 3-7, 9abα, 11-15, and dates it to the pre-monarchical period.

 80. Besides these there are some minor additions in vv. 9.1-2, 17a (ביום השלישי), 17b, 23bβ (וחטבי עצים ושאבי מים), 27 (which modifies the Gibeonites' duty to serve *for the altar* of Yahweh מזבח יהוה).

 81. J.A. Soggin, *Joshua: A Commentary* (OTL; London: SCM Press, 1972), p. 111.

2. Analyses of the Texts in Joshua and Judges

> But as for the towns of these peoples that the Lord your God is giving you as an inheritance, you must not let anything that breathes remain alive. You shall annihilate them (Deut. 20.16-17).[82]

Laws of warfare are not followed but, moreover, opposed through an illustration which shows that the principle of total annihilation is not agreed on every occasion and by all of the writers in DtrG. The aim of the writer is to prove that on some occasions it is acceptable for the foreigner to live among the Israelites and even to work in the temple, that is, the Gibeonites are an example of a foreign ethnic group which is allowed to have permanent and close relations with the Israelites. The Gibeonites may have been an acute and real historical dilemma during the time of writing, or they may just represent other ethnic groups in general. The latter case would mean, however, strong ideological criticism of deuteronomistic theology.

The theological perspective of the first deuteronomistic writer, totally fulfilled conquest, makes it hard to locate the earliest layer of ch. 9 to DtrH.[83] This understanding grows from the content of the chapter and is supported also by the observation that the *whole of ch. 9* as well as the follow-up in ch. 10 are just loosely connected into their literary context, and very probably belong to a large secondary insertion.[84] When the theological background for this literary layer is sought the following criteria should be fulfilled: the writer knows the deuteronomistic theology, especially the laws of warfare; the writer represents a tolerant ideology towards the other ethnic groups or at least towards one group; and finally is dated between the deuteronomistic writers (at least after DtrH) and P-stream. The theological stress thus points clearly away from the deuteronomistic writers.

The second text layer in ch. 9 confirms the peace agreement and

---

82. According to A. Rofé, 'The Laws of Warfare in the Book of Deuteronomy: Their Origin, Intent and Positivity', *JSOT* 32 (1985), pp. 23-44 (29-30), Deut 20.15-18 belong to the later section of laws.

83. Even in Josh. 11.19 (DtrH) the mention of Gibeonites is added afterwards, proved by the omission in the Septuagint.

84. In Josh. 10 one must count vv. 1b-2, 4aβb, 5bβ-6 in the secondary text layer. More detailed in K. Latvus, 'From Army Campsite to Partners in Peace: The Changing Role of the Gibeonites in the Redaction Process of Josh. x 1-8; xi 19', in K.-D. Schunk and M. Augustin (eds.), *'Lasset uns Brücken bauen ... ' Collected Communications to the XVth Congress of the International Organization for the Study of the Old Testament, Cambridge 1995* (BEATAJ, 42; Frankfurt am Main: Peter Lang, 1998), pp. 111-15.

gives a prominent theological label saying that Joshua did not just make peace with the Gibeonites but also a treaty (v. 15 ויכרת להם ברית), which was explicitly forbidden in Deut. 7.1-2, 'Make no covenant with them' (לא תכרת להם ברית). This layer also stays unidentified.

Social and Theological Background of Divine Anger
In the third text layer that belongs to the P-stream the issue is handled once more but from the new point of view, now also related to divine wrath. The focus of the writer is not to discharge Joshua from the responsibility[85] or to share the responsibility with the leaders, but to answer the inquiry 'Why was the peace agreement and the treaty not cancelled?' There might have been a real pressure 'to attack Gibeonites' (v. 18) but that was excluded using the idea of the oath sworn by the leaders.

An oath 'sworn by the Lord, God of Israel' was not comparable with a promise or a peace agreement because an oath was deeply connected with the cult and more generally with the God who was seen as guarantor of the oath and all promises related to it.[86] This meant that an oath was not only sworn to human beings but also to the God whose divine judgment was followed when the promises of the oath were not fulfilled.

> ... for every oath contained an implicit selfcurse which it was universally believed would result in direct divine action should that oath prove false. [...] Thus every oath (שבועה) carried an implicit אלה, which if that oath was broken or false, would automatically come into effect.[87]

On the other hand, the writer points out that the leaders ignored the requirement to 'ask direction from the Lord' (v. 14) which led to the theological dead end: the Israelites should have destroyed their enemies according to the warfare laws but obligations of the oath sworn in the name of Yahweh prevented that.

The analysis shows that the question about what attitude the Israelites should take to the Gibeonites was burning during the exile (dating of the first layer?) as well as during the postexilic period. All the layers more or less support the status given to the Gibeonites and

---

85. So Mayes, 'Deuteronomy 29', p. 321.
86. M.H. Pope, *Oath*, *IDB*, III, pp. 575-57; C.A. Keller, 'שבע ni. schwören', *THAT*, II, pp. 855-63.
87. A. Phillips, *Ancient Israel's Criminal Law: A New Approach to the Decalogue* (Oxford: Basil Blackwell, 1970), pp. 53, 55.

2. Analyses of the Texts in Joshua and Judges 69

show that at least this one foreign ethnic group has permission to stay and work among the Israelites, even in the temple. Does this interest have any connections to the historical information which we have about the Gibeonites?

According to the book of Joshua, Gibeon (current *el-Jib*) was sparsely inhabited before the thirteenth century BCE but flourished during the years 1200–600, having among other things large-scale wine production. While the population decreased sharply Gibeon stayed inhabited until the Roman period.[88] Archaeological excavations give some hints about the religious background in the town, exploring Yahweh-derived names (Hananiah, Asarjah, Amarjah, Hissiljah) as well as 54 fertility statues or objects from the Iron Age. The latter does not exclude the former but shows the plurality of religious practices.[89] References in the Old Testament show that the Gibeonites took part in the life of the community before exile (Jer. 28, the prophet Hananiah in the temple) or in the postexilic era (Neh. 3.7, the Gibeonites building the Jerusalem wall) without any special references to their ethnic background.

It is quite possible that the role of the Gibeonites was critical in the exilic/postexilic period for one reason or another. Their role might have changed or the rebuilding and reorganizing of the temple may have triggered a tension around the Gibeonites. In Joshua 9 the function of the Gibeonites in the temple is regulated several times: in the first layer as servants in the temple (v. 23) and then in the P-layer as 'hewers of wood and drawers of water for all the congregation' (v. 21). This shows that there was a continuing reason to reformulate the status of Gibeonites. Very probably the Gibeonites had a recognized status as lower labour personnel in the cult community[90]

---

88. J.B. Pritchard, *Gibeon's History in the Light of Excavations* (VTSup, 7; Leiden: E.J. Brill, 1959), p. 10; *idem*, *Gibeon Where the Sun Stood Still: The Discovery of the Biblical City* (Princeton, NJ: Princeton University Press, 1962), pp. 151-64; J. Blenkinsopp, *Gibeon and Israel: The Role of Gibeon and the Gibeonites in the Political and Religious History of Early Israel* (SOTSMS, 2; Cambridge: Cambridge University Press, 1972), p. 6; Kathleen M. Kenyon, *Archaeology in the Holy Land* (London: Ernest Benn; New York: W.W. Norton, 4th edn, 1979), pp. 328-29; AEHL, pp. 157-58.

89. About findings see Pritchard, *Gibeon*, pp. 120-21. About the pre-exilic religious development see G.W. Ahlström, 'An Archaeological Picture of Iron Age Religions in Ancient Palestine', *StudOr* 55 (1984), pp. 115-45 (122-24).

90. Blenkinsopp, *Gibeon*, pp. 98-108; see also Soggin, *Joshua*, pp. 112-13.

but their position was also threatened or even attacked by 'the congregation' (cf. v. 18).

All the time we should take into consideration that the Gibeonites in this story can actually be merely representatives of a foreign ethnic group among the Israelites. Hence each time 'Gibeonites' appear in the text, they could stand for any anonymous ethnic group (or groups) which caused this kind of ideological debate in the Persian period.

Wrath as a Symbol of Divine Order
The third writer of the chapter (P-stream) legitimates the whole procedure by threatening God's anger if the Israelites break the sworn oath. In Joshua 9, as in Joshua 22, the anger of God belongs to the sphere of priestly theology. The reason for anonymous divine anger[91] is no longer idolatry as in the deuteronomistic texts but breaking of the oath sworn in the name of Yahweh. The question of divine anger belongs with Yahweh religion, as in Joshua 22. The reason for leaving the anger without an explicit subject could be related to a more transcendental concept of God or to an unwillingness to speak about the anger of Yahweh in plain words.

The writer has used the idea of an oath as a theological key to close the case and show that all objections against the tolerant policy are useless—divine and anonymous anger is finally protecting the oath. To be more precise, against the background of the fifth-century social world the writer is calming down the discussion, 'a murmur' (v. 18), against the existing decision to guarantee the Gibeonites' position among the Israelites in temple service.

The anger of God has a new function as a divine protector of decisions made by leaders of the community. Here we can find also a connection between the use of anger in Joshua 22 and Joshua 9 because on both occasions the leaders give advice to the people or 'congregation' on how to act, and on both occasions there is a threat of wrath which is not, however, actualized. Divine wrath represents on both occasions the ultimate divine order which is materialized in the policy of the leaders.

---

91. Other appearances of anonymous divine anger in the Old Testament are Num. 1.53 and 18.5 (both P), Josh. 22.20 (P stream), 2 Kgs 3.27; 2 Chron. 19.10; 24.18; 32.25. See also the later influence in 1 Macc. 1.64 and Mt. 3.7; 1 Thess. 1.10; 2.16; 5.9.

Chapter 3

THE ANGER OF GOD IN DEUTERONOMY
AND IN THE PRIESTLY WRITINGS

The present study concentrates on the theme of the anger of God in the books of Joshua and Judges and, when possible, locates the theme within the historical context. It is possible to shed some more light on the issue through finding it on a larger scale in Deuteronomy and in the Priestly Writings.

A synopsis about the main themes of Deuteronomy and the basic results concerning the anger theme in the rest of the DtrG is needed not only for testing and comparing the results but also for creating larger theological frames around the anger theme.

1. The Anger of God in Deuteronomy, 1–2 Samuel and 1–2 Kings

The following summary is based on the mapping of the main results of the investigation for creating a general view of how the anger theme is located and dated in the rest of the DtrG. The idea about the growing process of the text or redaction-critical views of the researchers are also used if possible. Naturally the solutions are not unanimous but the following synopsis tries to find a consensus or majority opinion among the scholars.

To the basic text layer, DtrH,[1] scholars have located only a smaller proportion of passages that handle the anger theme in the DtrG. In Deuteronomy just two passages in the historical prologue, vv. 1.27, 34 (3.26?), come from the pen of DtrH;[2] one in the books of Samuel, in

1. Naturally the abbreviation DtrH is not used in all of the quoted studies but it stands for the first text layer.
2. Among others Steuernagel, *Das Deuteronomium* (1923), pp. 53-55, 63-64; S. Mittmann, *Deuteronomium 1I–63 literarkritisch und traditionsgeschichtlich untersucht* (BZAW, 139; Berlin: W. de Gruyter, 1975), pp. 165, 171; Preuss, *Deuteronomium*, p. 46. Cf. L. Perlitt, *Deuteronomium* (BKAT, 5.2; Neukirchen–Vluyn:

the appendix of 2 Sam. 24.1(?);[3] and two in the books of Kings, 1 Kgs 16.26 (?) and 22.54 (16.33?).[4] Besides these, 2 Sam. 6.7 has been seen as a piece of tradition material added by DtrH.

Nevertheless, it is very difficult to find a meaningful connection between these passages because the motive of anger differs greatly. Perhaps there is a loose common theme somehow related to abandoning or giving up Yahweh, but even then passages in Samuel are connected more closely to the taboo issue (2 Sam. 6.7) or non-motivated anger (2 Sam. 24.1). Clearly the anger theme does not belong to the core of DtrH, and moreover nearly all of the identifications raise question marks, especially 2 Sam. 24.1, 1 Kgs 16.26 and 22.54, which might be the work of the later writer.

Also the few passages which have been identified with the DtrP (1 Kgs 14.9; 16.2; 21.22)[5] focus the motive of the anger of Yahweh more clearly around one central topic: judgment oracles which are directed against the dynasties because they have worshipped other gods. Identification of two other passages (1 Sam. 28.18?;[6] 2 Kgs 23.19?[7]) is not so obvious and also the grounds of the anger differ

---

Neukirchener Verlag, 1991), pp. 102-105 (1.27 belongs to the basic text; 1.34 to the later insertion).

3. Veijola, *Die ewige Dynastie*, p. 84.

4. See Würthwein, *Die Bücher* (1985), pp. 196-201, 265; G.H. Jones, *1 and 2 Kings* (2 vols.; NCB; Grand Rapids: Eerdmans; London: Marshall, Morgan & Scott, 1984), pp. 372, 375. Cf. B. Stade and F. Schwally, *The Books of Kings: Critical Edition of the Hebrew Text* (SBOT, 9; Leipzig: J.C. Hinrichs, 1904), pp. 22-23: 16.26b (addition); Dietrich, *Prophetie*, p. 136: 16.33 (DtrH); Spieckermann, *Juda*, pp. 207-208: 16.33 (DtrN).

5. Dietrich, *Prophetie*, pp. 53-54, 59-60, 89-90; Würthwein, *Die Bücher* (1985), pp. 174, 194-95, and *Die Bücher* (1984), p. 251.

6. DtrP: Veijola, *Die ewige Dynastie*, pp. 57-58; W. Dietrich, *David, Saul und die Propheten: Das Verhältnis von Religion und Politik nach den prophetischen Überlieferungen vom frühesten Königtum in Israel* (BWANT, 122; Stuttgart: W. Kohlhammer, 1987), p. 35 (against his earlier decision). DtrN: Dietrich, *Prophetie*, p. 86. Foresti, *The Rejection of Saul*, pp. 87-88; M. Nissinen, *Prophetie, Redaktion und Fortschreibung im Hoseabuch: Studien zum Werdegang eines Prophetenbuches im Lichte von Hos 4 und 11* (AOAT, 231; Kevelaer: Butzon & Bercker; Neukirchen–Vluyn: Neukirchener Verlag, 1991), p. 328.

7. DtrP: Dietrich, *Prophetie*, pp. 117-20. Spieckermann, *Juda*, pp. 116-19. Late insertion: R. Kittel, *Die Bücher der Könige* (HKAT, 1.5; Göttingen: Vandenhoeck & Ruprecht, 1900), p. 297; A.F. Puukko, *Das Deuteronomium: Eine literarkritische*

3. The Anger of God in Deuteronomy

from Saul's disobedience to transgression against centralization laws of the cult.

The largest proportion of the anger passages have been identified with the late deuteronomistic layer (DtrN, DtrB, exilic dtr, etc.). In Deuteronomy there are 27 passages (Deut. 1.37; 4.21, 25; 6.15; 7.4; 9.7, 8, 18, 19, 20, 22, 28; 11.17; 12.31; 13.18; 16.22; 29.19, 22, 23, 26, 27; 31.17, 29; 32.16, 19, 21, 22)[8] which scholars almost unanimously locate within the later part of the deuteronomistic movement. This information illustrates the present consensus of scholars that the anger theme did not belong to the pre-exilic deuteronomic law codex but was really a (late-) deuteronomistic invention. In 1–2 Kings there are 15 passages which are located to the similar level: 1 Kgs 8.46; 11.9; 14.15; 15.30; 16.7; 2 Kgs 13.3; 17.11, 17, 18; 21.6, 15; 22.13, 17, 26; 24.20.[9]

Untersuchung (Leipzig: J.C. Hinrichs', 1909), p. 10; Würthwein, *Die Bücher* (1984), pp. 454, 460-61 (post-dtr).

8. Classification to the late deuteronomistic stage is based on the majority decisions of the following studies. For details see the corresponding passages. Steuernagel, *Das Deuteronomium* (1923); Mittmann, *Deuteronomium*; Preuss, *Deuteronomium*; Perlitt, *Deuteronomium*; Mayes, *The Story*; D. Knapp, *Deuteronomium 4: Literarische Analyse und theologische Interpretation* (GTA, 35; Göttingen: Vandenhoeck & Ruprecht, 1987); E. Aurelius, *Der Fürbitter Israels: Eine Studie zum Mosebild im Alten Testament* (ConBOT, 27; Lund: Almqvist & Wiksell, 1988); N. Lohfink, *Das Hauptgebot: Eine Untersuchung literarischer Einleitungsfragen zu Dtn 5–11* (AnBib 20; Rome: Pontificio Istituto Biblico, 1963); T. Veijola, 'Bundestheologische Redaktion im Deuteronomium', in *idem* (ed.), *Das Deuteronomium und seine Querbeziehungen* (SESJ, 62; Helsinki: Finnische Exegetische Gesellschaft; Göttingen: Vandenhoeck & Ruprecht, 1996), pp. 242-76. A larger survey of the results in K. Latvus, *Jumalan viha: Redaktiokriittinen tutkimus Joosuan ja Tuomarien kirjojen jumalakuvasta* (SESJ, 58; Helsinki: The Finnish Exegetical Society, 1993), pp. 29-52.

9. The classification to the late deuteronomistic stage is based on the majority decisions of the following studies. For details see the corresponding passages: Jones, *1 and 2 Kings*; Würthwein, *Die Bücher* (1984) and *Die Bücher* (1985); Dietrich, *Prophetie*; Jepsen, *Die Quellen*, and *idem*, 'Ahabs Busse: Ein kleiner Beitrag zur Methode literarhistorischer Einordnung', in A. Kuschke and E. Kutsch (eds.), *Archäologie und Altes Testament* (Festschrift K. Galling; Tübingen: J.C.B. Mohr, 1970), pp. 145-55; Šanda, *Die Bücher*; G. Hentschel, *2 Könige* (Die Neue Echter Bibel; Kommentar zum Alten Testament mit der Einheitsübersetzung, 11; Stuttgart: Echter Verlag, 1985). See also Nelson, *The Double Redaction*; Provan, *Hezekiah*. A larger survey of the results in Latvus, *Jumalan viha*, pp. 29-52.

Thus there are in total 42 late deuteronomistic passages about the anger of God in the whole DtrG (excluding Joshua and Judges) which explain how giving up Yahweh and worshipping other gods provoked the anger of Yahweh against the Israelites. To this rule there are two exceptions: 1 Kgs 8.46 (to sin) and 2 Kgs 24.20 (no reason at all). Very often the anger causes historical or national crises, troubles and wars which are obviously symbols of the main disaster: exile.

Post-deuteronomistic identifications among the anger expressions in DtrG are exceptional in the earlier studies.

2. *Hidden Anger among the Main Themes of Deuteronomy*

Following mapping of the main themes of Deuteronomy reveals theological frames of the anger theme inside deuteronomistic theology. Caused by the diversity of the literary material in Deuteronomy scholars have not presented just one major theme but more like a cluster of themes, partially overlapping each other. Instead of going through all of them, half a dozen different views have been chosen to represent the variety of opinions.

According to *C. Steuernagel* there are six major theological areas or themes in Deuteronomy: (1) Yahweh is the only God in Israel, jealously forbidding the worship of other gods, (2) Yahweh is the kind and loving God of Israel, (3) absolute demand of the law (especially against other nations), (4) broad-minded cultic understanding, (5) ethical demand which (6) shows that 'the law of Deuteronomy expresses truly a prophetic law'.[10]

In his study about the theological traditions of Israel *G. von Rad* locates the origin and use of Deuteronomy to the festival were the covenant was renewed in Shechem (*Bundeserneuerungsfest*) and found its final form in the continuing sermon activities of the Levites,[11] who especially presented a call for obedience to the laws of Yahweh. The call was based on the deeds Yahweh had done in history and therefore Yahweh should be loved 'with all your heart, and with all soul, and with all your might' (Deut. 6.5). The cult should be centralized in one place to protect it against the Canaanite Baal-cult; however, the theological seeking after the will of God was not to be limited to the cult,

---

10. Steuernagel, *Lehrbuch*, pp. 200-203.
11. Von Rad, *Theologie*, pp. 233-34.

3. *The Anger of God in Deuteronomy* 75

but instead expressed as a holistic demand concerning the life of Israel.[12]

The central themes of Deuteronomy can be expressed in three views according to *S. Herrmann*. They are as follows: limiting the cult to one place (*Kultuseinheit*); the purity of the cult, that is, rejecting other gods (*Kultusreinheit*); and addressing the demands to the whole of Israel.[13]

H.D. Preuss sums up the theology of Deuteronomy in four headlines: (1) God and service (Yahweh is the only God who is served in one place and simultaneously keeps social responsibilities in mind), (2) Israel (how to live as God's nation), (3) the history of Israel (the historical roots of the people of God which have to be remembered to receive the blessing), (4) the land of Israel (promises to the ancestors concentrated on the possession as well as the present threats of losing the land) and (5) law and obedience (the relation between Yahweh and the Israelites requires the fulfilment of the obligation).[14]

O. Kaiser expresses the corresponding theological programme in one sentence: 'One nation in front of one God, chosen from all nations of the world, united in cult in a place chosen by God and called in obedience to love and fear God in a land which God has given.' Yahweh has chosen Israel and created the relation which is based on love and a one-sided promise (*Selbstverpflichtung*). Although the core of Deuteronomy is a law codex it should not be mixed with legalism (*Gesetzlichkeit*) because the choice precedes the law. Obedience to the law is 'an answer to God's salvation acts and the consequence of loving and fearing God'.[15]

Worth mentioning also is the synthesis produced by *R.E. Clements* which can be condensed into the four titles: God (only to be worshipped), Israel (the chosen nation), worship (in one place) and social justice.[16]

---

12. Von Rad, *Theologie*, pp. 236-42.
13. S. Herrmann, 'Die konstruktive Restauration: Das Deuteronomium als Mitte biblischer Theologie', in H.W. Wolff (ed.), *Probleme biblischer Theologie* (Festschrift G. von Rad; Munich: Chr. Kaiser Verlag, 1971), pp. 155-70 (158-59).
14. Preuss, *Deuteronomium*, pp. 174-201.
15. O. Kaiser, *Einleitung in das Alte Testament: Eine Einführung in ihre Ergebnisse und Probleme* (Gütersloh: Gerd Mohn, 5th edn, 1984), pp. 136-37.
16. R.E. Clements, *Deuteronomy* (OTG; Sheffield: Sheffield Academic Press, 1989), pp. 49-67.

Between Love and Anger
The preceding short introduction to the main elements of the theology of Deuteronomy was not detailed but concentrated on the slogans. Nevertheless, it is meaningful because in the middle of these catchwords and main themes we are seeking the soil from which the theology of anger grows.

According to former investigations the main themes of Deuteronomy can be summed up in four points: centralization of the cult, Israel as the people of Yahweh, Yahweh as the only God of the Israelites and the demand to obey the law. The crystallization of deuteronomistic theology can be found in Deut. 6.5: 'You shall love the Lord your God with all your heart, and with all your soul, and with all your might.'

One of the main results for the present study is that the anger of God was *not* mentioned among the central themes but instead the love of God appears. The love between God and the Israelites occurs several times in Deuteronomy—7 times Yahweh is the subject, 12 times the people are.[17] Comparing these statistics with anger expressions the result is clear: anger beats love by four to one.

The basic anger theology in Joshua and Judges, and in the rest of the DtrG alike, has used in a stereotypical way the central concepts and the structure of deuteronomistic theology: Forsake Yahweh—Serve other gods—Anger of Yahweh will be kindled—People will face an accident, that means, exile. When we compare the basic structure of dtr-theology with the structure of the dtr-theology of anger, the connection becomes obvious:

1. Love Yahweh	1. Forsake Yahweh
2. Serve only Yahweh	2. Serve other gods
3. Yahweh will bless his people	3. The anger of Yahweh will be kindled
4. People can use the fruits of the land	4. People will face an accident, i.e. exile

Both structures deal with the same question of the relationship between Yahweh and the people of the Israel, and give negative and positive answers.[18] The same dual form of expression is also used in Neo-Assyrian treaties, which probably had a decisive influence on the language of deuteronomistic theology (cf. Josh. 23).

17. Yahweh as a subject: 4.37; 7.8, 13; 10.15, 18; 15.16; 23.6. People as a subject: 5.10; 6.5; 7.9; 10.12; 11.1, 13, 22; 13.4; 19.9; 30.6, 16, 20.
18. Cf. H. Spieckermann, 'Barmherzig und gnädig ist der Herr...', *ZAW* 102 (1990), pp. 1-18 (6).

3. *The Anger of God in Deuteronomy*

Why have the former investigations ignored anger and chosen love? Probably the answer can be found in the customers: those who read theology have more use for love but the anger of God in the middle of the theological structures could cause a lot of inconvenience for modern theologians. Presumably scholars have just unconsciously used ideological criticism and ignored the anger.

After all, the double view, to be blessed by God or to be hit by the anger of God, does belong to the core of deuteronomistic theology. Just as the rise and blossoming of the Israelite nation are part of the deuteronomistic agenda in a corresponding way the theology of anger forms the way of destruction. The love of God and anger of God are mirror images of each other, both being part of the core of deuteronomistic theology—another question is whether this belongs any more to the centre of modern theological synthesis.

3. *The Priestly Writings: Anger in the Postexilic Power Struggle*

The analysis in Joshua 9 and 22 showed that the latest text layers were closely related to the Priestly movement and followed different theological patterns also in the anger theme. These results can be evaluated by surveying the theme of the anger of God in the Priestly Writings which can be rather confidently identified in the Pentateuch and dated to the exilic/postexilic period according to the clear majority of scholars. Further, the heterogeneous literary character as well as the division of the basic text (P^g) and later additions (P^s) is largely agreed.[19] P-texts—which on several occasions seem to supplement the deuteronomistic literary activities—probably represent a movement or a party which was at least partly contemporary and even a competing group with the deuteronomistic circle.

Already a short look at the vocabulary used in P to describe the anger of God shows a great difference from deuteronomistic theology: the words חמה 'heat, rage, burning anger' (Lev. 26.28), and קצף 'anger' (Num. 1.53; 17.11; 18.5), קצף 'be wroth' (Lev. 10.6; Num. 16.22), are used in P to describe the anger of God. Also the comparison of the numbers of occurrences illustrates the difference: in DtrG

---

19. About the content and dating see Noth, *Überlieferungsgeschichte*, pp. 8-11, 17-20; Smend, *Die Entstehung*, pp. 47-50, 57; Kaiser, *Einleitung*, pp. 112-17; Hayes, *An Introduction*, p. 194.

the theme of the anger of God appears nearly 10 times more often than in P.

Continued Disobedience (Leviticus 26)

Among all other P appearances Lev. 26.28 is a special case because it is part of the so-called Holiness Code and with ch. 26 is a very close parallel to Deuteronomy 28, both describing a duality of life between the ways of blessing and curse. If the Israelites choose the way of blessing and follow God's statutes (חקת) and keep his commandments (מצות) God will give them prosperity in every part of life (vv. 3-13). On the other hand, disobedience to the will of God will cause a deepening series of punishments (vv. 16-39) which will not end before the collective confession of sin.[20]

The anger of God in v. 28 is located in the last section of the curses (vv. 27-33) which are crystallized in a total destruction of the cities in Palestine and in the dispersion of the Israelites among the nations, a similar structure as in deuteronomistic theology. Despite these similarities Leviticus 26 has its own characteristics, especially the idea of the desolated land which needs the rest of the Sabbath.

Further, the fundamental reason for the anger of God grows from different soil since idolatry is not the central issue in the chapter, and even when the prohibition regarding making statues of other gods is mentioned in vv. 1-2 it remains just an isolated item without any relation to the anger theme. Moreover, the latter part of the chapter is structured with the blame that Israelites 'continue to be hostile' (תלכו עמי קרי vv. 21, 23, 27, 40) to God and this is first responded to in a similar way by God (הלכתי עמכם בקרי vv. 24) but finally emphasized with the anger theme in v. 28: 'I will continue to be hostile to you *in fury*' (הלכתי עמכם בחמת קרי). Fury or anger thus represents the ultimate reaction of God. Bitter desolation is not, however, the final focus of the passage: repentance and the renewed covenant between God and the Israelites.

The anger theme in the Holiness Code is just a distant echo from the deuteronomistic anger theology, except that the burning issue about worshipping other gods is replaced with a more general concept of

---

20. See more detailed discussion in A. Cholewinski, *Heiligkeitsgesetz und Deuteronomium: Eine vergleichende Studie* (AnBib, 66; Rome: Biblical Institute Press, 1976), pp. 310-19; K. Elliger, *Leviticus* (HAT, 4; Tübingen: J.C.B. Mohr, 1966), p. 371.

3. *The Anger of God in Deuteronomy* 79

disobedience to God, as in a late deuteronomistic passage 1 Kgs 8.46.[21] The anger of God is a symbol of breaking the relation between Yahweh and the Israelites, followed by the end of the nation.

Holiness as Anger (Leviticus 10.1-7; Numbers 1.48-54; 18.1-7)
The following passages, Lev. 10.6, Num. 1.53 and 18.5, present a completely new way of thinking in relation to the anger theme, namely, they refer to the possibility that the anger of God is turned against the people because of the failures of cult personnel. Each story has in the background the notion of God's ultimate holiness (Lev. 10.3), which requires both total obedience and strict division between the sacred and profane worlds. Those who are dedicated to the sacred world have a responsibility to protect others from direct contact with the holy (Num. 1.53; 18.4-5).

The description of the inauguration of the offering cult in the basic story in P (Lev. 9) ends with the appearance of the glory of Yahweh (כבוד יהוה) as a fire 'consuming the burnt offering and the fat on the altar'. Surprisingly this is followed by the dark chapter about Nadab and Abihu who bring somehow unholy or wrong fire to the altar— only to be annihilated by the fire sent by Yahweh.

The enigmatic passage Lev. 10.1-7 which seems to be a later supplement within the P movement (PS)[22] does not even give a reason why foreign or unholy fire (אש זרה) was forbidden. Such an activity was simply 'not commanded' by Yahweh (לא צוה אתם), that is, it did not happen according to the holy order which should have been followed in detail.

The unexpected death of Nadab and Abihu is not honoured with normal mourning rites but, on the contrary, in vv. 6-7 the priests are explicitly not allowed to mourn unlike the lay people (v. 6b). The latter is likely to be a secondary addition just to soften an otherwise too strict story. Probably the mourning rites of the priests could be interpreted as a sign of sympathy for those who had broken the sacred order or even as a protest against God's judgment because the mourning would threaten the existence of the whole community: 'you

---

21. W. Thiel, 'Erwägungen zum Alter des Heiligkeitsgesetzes', *ZAW* 81 (1969), pp. 40-73 (67).

22. Noth, *Überlieferungsgeschichte*, pp. 19, 204; N. Lohfink, *Die Priesterschrift und die Geschichte* (VTSup, 29; Leiden: E.J. Brill, 1978), p. 198; Aurelius, *Der Fürbitter*, p. 189.

will die and the wrath will strike all the congregation' (v. 6a). The wrath is not defined any closer nor is its subject mentioned but the context reveals that it is a question about divine anger, as in Joshua 9 and 22.

Thus it is obvious that the anger of God in the P movement is closely related to the question about the sacred and holy. Even a minor mistake in holy orders can be judged without any further warnings and without any possibility of complaining about the decisions. God revealed in fire, death and wrath belongs to the transcendental world which strongly stresses the division between sacral and profane, and also the seriousness that is needed to follow cult orders. Actually divine anger and holiness are nearly synonymous on this occasion.

The passage Num. 1.48-54 follows the same theme when special orders are given to the Levites to camp around the tabernacle of the covenant 'that there may be no wrath on the congregation of the Israelites' (v. 53 ולא יהיה קצף על עדת בני ישראל). Verses 48-54 are also a later insertion to P.[23]

Verse 53 illustrates Priestly understanding of the anger of God: the reason for the anger is not idolatry nor even a cultic wrong deed but the direct contact between God and the Israelites. Actually the Israelites do not even need to contact Yahweh to be under threat but merely to enter the sacred environment. The correspondence of human and divine threat is obvious because the Levites not only protect the Israelites from touching the holy but they are also ordered to annihilate invaders: 'Any outsider who comes near shall be put to death' (v. 51).

According to the P movement, the sacredness of the cult environment is based on the holiness of God which prevents ordinary people from crossing the line between everyday life and the transcendence of God. Cult personnel are both protecting other people from the holy wrath of God and also ensuring that the holy environment is not defiled.

The third similar passage in P is in Num. 18.1-7, which gives the Levites an established status in cult service but at the same time classifies them as lower cult personnel who are not allowed to

---

23. Noth, *Überlieferungsgeschichte*, p. 19; D. Kellermann, *Die Priesterschrift von Numeri 1_1 bis 10_{10} literarkritisch und traditionsgeschichtlich untersucht* (BZAW, 120; Berlin: W. de Gruyter, 1970), pp. 25-32.

approach the altar. When all the duties of the sanctuary and altar are performed in an appropriate way and all outsiders are kept away from the sacred world, divine 'wrath may never again come upon the Israelites' (v. 5 ולא יהיה עוד קצף על בני ישראל). As with the others above, this section is also unanimously classified to be a later supplement to P.[24]

To sum up: anger is a manifestation of God's holiness, which should not be disturbed by those who belong to the non-sacred sphere of life, but also breaking the taboo-rules can arouse God's anger against those who bring 'unholy fire' to the altar or enter into the sacred sphere. Even mourning for those who have met God's holiness is forbidden. What can be the literary, theological and social background of these passages? All three occurrences follow more or less the same pattern, all belonging to the Priestly movement and being later supplements from a literary point of view, but in addition they may also reflect contemporary theological changes in the policy of cult practices in postexilic Judaism. Clearly they strive to confine the people who have the right of entry to the sacred world and have access to the altar while others are labelled as 'outsiders' (זר). This division is secured with divine authority, holiness and wrath. In other words, this concept of god with its transcendence and holiness legitimates the status of the priesthood as well as the status and position of the lower classes of the cult personnel, the Levites. This kind of new formulation of the rights of the different religious groups may also have been controversial:

> Here both reform groups [reform priests and deuteronomistic oriented lay theologians] came together in their concern to establish a self-administered community without royal supervision. However, conflicts inevitably broke out over how far the priestly selfadministration of the cult should go and whether it excluded the collaboration of the laity.[25]

The serious and bitter nature of this conflict can be seen in the last P section which is related to the anger theme: Numbers 16–17.

The Anger of God as an Instrument of Power Struggle (Numbers 16–17)

The main issue in the literarily heterogeneous section Numbers 16–17 is the leadership of the community, or, to be more precise, criticism

---

24. Noth, *Das vierte Buch Mose*, pp. 118-19: 'Sprachlich und sachlich gehört das Stück in die Spätzeit'; Smend, *Die Entstehung*, p. 48.
25. Albertz, *A History*, II, p. 485.

of Moses and Aaron, the leaders of the cult community, which arouses the anger of God (16.22 קצף). Finally, people's protests against the fate of the critics only provoke God to greater anger (17.11 קצף) and destruction among the Israelites. As a matter of fact, in chs. 16–17 there is a series of conflicts where first the group of Korah and then people led by Dathan and Abiram want to confront their political and religious leaders. The common fate among all these groups is total annihilation—the earth swallows or divine fire consumes them—and finally, a large section of the congregation gathered to protest these unfair events face their end by plague.

The earliest literary layer in Numbers 16–17 is the Dathan-Abiram episode which has been identified with the Yahwistic writer (J)[26] or with the postexilic deuteronomistic writer.[27] This layer does not yet mention Aaron or deal with the question about the priesthood but focuses on the position of Moses as a leader, and instead of the anger of God it mentions the anger of Moses (16.15). The layer contains probably vv. 1-2a*, 12-15, 25-26, 27b-34 (not 32b). Transition to confrontation between priests and lay people or between priests and lower cult personnel Levites becomes acute in later supplementary layers which belong to the priestly texts (P^S).[28]

The earliest priestly layer, already P^S, contained the protest of Korah and 250 *lay people* against the position of Moses and Aaron (vv. 16.3-7a, 18*, (19-24?, 27a?,) 35; 17.6-15).[29] One of the key arguments against the priestly hegemony in the community is that 'All the congregation are holy, everyone of them, and the Lord is among them. So why then do you exalt yourselves above the assembly of the Lord?' (v. 3).

The solution concerning holiness and divine authorization is found when all the men took their censers with incense 'and the fire came out from the Lord and consumed' them. The sequel to the story (17.6-15) does not leave any space for re-evaluation of the divine sentence

26. Wellhausen, *Die Composition*, pp. 102-105; O. Eissfeldt, *Hexateuch-Synopse: Die Erzählung der fünf Bücher Mose und des Buches Josua mit dem Anfang des Richterbuches* (repr.; Darmstadt: Wissenschaftliche Buchgesellschaft, 1983), 63, 177*, 277* (pages asterisked in original); Noth, *Überlieferungsgeschichte*, p. 34.

27. Aurelius, *Der Fürbitter*, pp. 194-95.

28. Noth, *Überlieferungsgeschichte*, p. 19 n. 59; Smend, *Die Entstehung*, p. 48; Aurelius, *Der Fürbitter*, pp. 193-94. See also Albertz, *A History*, II, p. 633 n. 143.

29. See Noth, *Überlieferungsgeschichte*, p. 19; Eissfeldt, *Hexateuch-Synopse*, pp. 173-76*; Aurelius, *Der Fürbitter*, pp. 192-98 (without Korah).

because the wrath of God in the form of the plague strikes those who protested the fate of the 250 men. Only when Aaron made the atonement for the people were the rest saved, already a reflection of the final commitment to be the dedicated family in order to perform 'priestly duties in all that concerns the altar and the area behind the curtain' (Num. 18.7).

It is uncertain whether the rest of the texts in Numbers 16–17 (vv. 16.7b, 8-11, 16-17, 19-24, 32b; 17.1-5)[30] form one literary layer or if it is a question about a few separate additions, but the certain thing is that the status of the Korah group as Levites was introduced in this level (16.8-11). With this change the conflict between priests and lay people has been transposed to the conflict between two sacred groups.

When the Levites protest against the priests chosen by Yahweh they are also confronting God (v. 11), and in this way commit sin (v. 22) which leads to the anger of God against the whole congregation (v. 22 ועל כל העדה תקצף). Only the intercession of Moses and Aaron saves the community, excluding Korah and all belonging to him, for 'the earth opened its mouth and swallowed them up'.

Thus in the priestly texts a similar plot occurs twice: the position of the leaders is exposed to criticism by those who are out of power or denied privileges, God condemns them and only the priestly act saves the nation from total annihilation. Those who were criticized become the only defenders of the people which also seals their status as God's special mediators.

In previous analyses in Joshua 9 and 22 the priestly texts can be assumed to reflect inner conflicts of postexilic Judaism about who has the right to interpret the practical application of Jewish religion. The same is even more obvious in Numbers 16–17 where the competing groups are openly giving arguments and confronting their opponents.[31] Acute fights between the parties have been projected back into history and described, of course, from the winners' point of view. Thus the leaders in power tried to protect their position against attacks from

---

30. Compare Eissfeldt, *Hexateuch-Synopse*, pp. 173-76*; Aurelius, *Der Fürbitter*, pp. 192-98 (including all appearances of Korah). See also Albertz, *A History*, II, p. 633 n. 143.

31. Compare Noth, *Überlieferungsgeschichte*, p. 138; von Rad, *Theologie*, p. 303.

lower cult personnel or representatives of the people: lay-leaders.

According to the existing literary sources it is most likely that we are dealing with the conflict between reform priests and deuteronomistic-oriented lay theologians.[32] Those two major movements have strongly affected the content of Jewish canonical writings, both being active about the same time and lastly, the growing process of the texts show that the priestly writers had the last word in the editing process of historical texts. The early postexilic period actualized the questions when the temple was rededicated, some priestly groups returned from the exile/Diaspora and at the same period the late deuteronomistic movement interpreted monarchical promises to be reformulated in a 'democratic' spirit.[33] The activities of Ezrah and Nehemiah illustrate that in Babylonia there were also later in the fifth century individuals or groups who wanted to interfere in the life of the Jewish community in Palestine, and therefore we should not think of the end of the sixth century as the only possible period for these confrontations.

In the priestly party the divine anger was an effective instrument in the power struggle against other groups. Those who were opposing the priestly hegemony in the temple were reminded that the criticism itself, based on whatever arguments, was wrong and to be condemned. The final episode in Numbers 17 goes so far that it denies even the discussion about events. The priestly party very probably already had a leading position in the Jewish community and with the help of these stories about the anger of God they wanted to secure their status towards both the lay leaders and lower cult personnel raising themselves above criticism.

The trend which was in bud in priestly oriented texts of Joshua (chs. 9 and 22) blossoms in the Priestly part of the Pentateuch. The concept of God in the priestly texts related to the anger theme seems to be fully assimilated with politics and using the power against other Jewish parties. 'God' has become an instrument or weapon which can be manipulated for purposes of their own.

---

32. Cf. Nissinen, *Prophetie*, pp. 209-11 (about the similar confrontation in Hosea); Albertz, *A History*, II, pp. 486-88.

33. Veijola, *Die ewige Dynastie*, pp. 141-42; *idem*, *Verheissung in der Krise: Studien zur Literatur und Theologie der Exilzeit anhand des 89: Psalms* (AASF, Series B, 220; Helsinki: Academia Scientiarum Fennica, 1982), p. 173: 'Alles, was Gott David und seinen Nachkommen einst zugesagt hatte, sollte dem Volk Israel zugute kommen.'

Chapter 4

CONCLUSIONS AND IMPLICATIONS

1. *The Writing Process*

DtrH
The text of DtrH has proved to be narrower than expected according to former investigations. A brief basic story which concentrated on the national leaders in the books of Joshua and Judges was the start of the long and complicated growth process. The following passages belong to DtrH in the texts reflected in this study: Josh. 1.1-2, 10-11... 7.2-5; 8.1-29*; 10.1a, 3-4aα, 5abα, 7-43*... 21.43-45; 24*; Judg. 2.7-11a, 14b-16a (no 15aβ), 18aβb; 3.7aα, 8aβ-11... 10.1-5, 17-18; 11.1-40*. DtrH wants to emphasize that the Israelites as a nation were fully dependent on Yahweh and that the disasters which they had met were useful for realizing this relationship more deeply.

The victories and defeats of the early national period prepare the plot for the major catastrophes (2 Kgs 17*; 24-25*) but the tone is not pessimistic because the national hardships do not mean dead ends but just learning experiences from DtrH's point of view. The aim of the story of DtrH is to teach the nation 'to know Yahweh' and 'the work that he had done for Israel' (Judg. 2.10).

Also worth mentioning is that DtrH does not even mention the anger of God in Joshua and Judges or the present polemic against the worship of other gods.

The Lack of DtrP
After DtrH but before the DtrN, writers that cannot be identified with DtrP have worked on some passages. The existence of these texts (Josh. 1.3-6; 23.1-5, 9b-10, 14), as well as the lack of the expected DtrP-texts, shows clearly that the tripartite redaction model (DtrH–DtrP–DtrN) is not the best one for investigating Joshua and Judges, and may also be misleading for the whole DtrG because the model

86   *God, Anger and Ideology*

ignores a large number of non-deuteronomistic writers who participated in the writing process.

DtrN
On one occasion (Judg. 2) it was proven that DtrN-texts were not made by a single writer but by a succession of writers, and the same can be assumed also in the other texts identified with the similar layer. DtrN had contributed significantly to making larger frames of the Judges stories and creating the theological overviews. The formerly used identification marks of the DtrN-group—the demand to obey the law and warnings from other nations—should be complemented with the idea of God's anger caused by worship of other gods.

From the Redaction to the Growing Process
The literary growing process did not end with dtr-redactors, but continued with priestly (some parts in Josh. 9; 22) and other post-deuteronomistic texts (Josh. 1.8-9; 1.12-18; 7.1, 9-26; 22.1-4, 5, 6). The best theory for understanding the birth of the DtrG is to lay more emphasis than previously upon a continuous literary growth and reinterpretation process (*Fortschreibung*), although the first writer (DtrH) should be considered as a typical redactor who collects sources and creates the story plot coloured with writers' theological views.

2. *The Anger of God*

Deuteronomistic Texts
In the text of DtrH the question of God's anger does not appear even once, although most of the basic elements of the deuteronomistic theology of anger are present. This was first made explicit by the editors of the DtrN-group, whose ideas can be compressed into the following points.

The reason for God's anger is idolatry which symbolizes in DtrN-theology a totally negative attitude to everything that God has done or given to the Israelites. Forgetting Yahweh and serving other gods, Israelites neglected the basic principles of life, namely, that they were fully dependent on Yahweh.

The theology of anger is deeply bound to experiences of national catastrophes and crises and ought to be evaluated only in this context. It can be called theology of experience because the values of the past

4. Conclusions and Implications

are interpreted in the light of historical events and experiences. In deuteronomistic theology, unlike later chronistic writings, experiences of individuals have no specific importance, which means that we are dealing with the collective experience of an exiled generation.

Connections to the historical traditions of the oriental environment in deuteronomistic writings can also be seen in the influence of the Neo-Assyrian covenant treaties. They offered a functioning way to demonstrate the relationship between Yahweh and his people, although the lack of direct quotations shows that deuteronomistic writers did not mechanically copy some Assyrian ideas or structures of political treaties but applied and reinterpreted them strongly.

The structures of DtrN-theology relate the concept of God to the question of justice. Exile represented the hard realities of life which were undeniable and so real that the whole idea about God as protector of Israel was threatened. Because they did not want to give up the idea of the powerful God who also guaranteed justice on Earth they had to rationalize the meaning of exile and say that it was caused by the anger of God which in turn was caused by the idolatry of the Israelites. This logic saved most of the traditional beliefs but made God's nature twofold: loving and wrathful.

The questions of the theology of anger and the demand to obey the law are connected with each other in the DtrN-group. DtrH motivated God's help through his mercy (Judg. 2.18b 'for the Lord would be moved to pity by their groaning') but the way of thinking had changed radically in Judg. 10.16 where the DtrN writer stresses the people's deeds as a condition for Yahweh's help.

Deuteronomistic theology pushed the guilt of national and historical events onto the shoulders of the Israelite people: their wrong religious attitudes and behaviour was the original reason for exile and only their repentance would restore the situation. Thus political, ideological and theological arguments seem to be strongly interwoven in the texts of DtrN.

Post-Deuteronomistic Texts
Post-deuteronomistic texts related to the anger of God turn the view from external threats and questions to the rigorous orders concerning how to serve Yahweh in the right way, in the right place and under the guidance of the right people.

Compared to DtrH and DtrN a more strict attitude to the law can be found in a later text, Joshua 7 (which is a combination of dtr, P and chronistic ideas), where Yahweh turns from his anger only after the stoning of Achan who had committed a theft. Changes in punishments mirror stricter attitudes in theology and in society in the postexilic period.

The priestly texts on their side give a wholly different view of the theology of anger. Among other things the anger of God has become an instrument in the power struggle between Jewish parties or the ultimate legitimization of the position of priestly leaders. In these cases writers have assimilated their own interpretations with God's will and created a system which cannot even be criticized by others without causing the risk of divine anger.

The development from the early deuteronomistic texts to the late priestly insertions illustrates how the concept of God always reflects contemporary historical and social questions as well as the pre-occupations of the writers and their ideological backgrounds. During the process the content in the concept of God has turned practically upside down: DtrH proclaimed God as a merciful helper of Israel but later writers made him either enemy of the people or supporter of one Israelite party against the others. The search for God in the Old Testament pages is also a survey of human interests.

An Uncritical Epilogue

IN SEARCH OF THE THEOLOGICAL INTENTION
BEYOND THE ANGER OF GOD

After finishing my doctoral thesis about the anger of God I was once asked by a friend of mine, himself a minister, 'You have an interesting topic. Could you explain what function the anger of God still has?' This simple question, probably shared by many other Christians, stopped me in my tracks because it showed that the results of academic study about the concept of God in the Bible trigger expectations that current beliefs about God be evaluated. Should I just ignore the problem which clearly went beyond my academic definitions and explain that I have merely concentrated on ancient texts and beliefs which may differ a lot from present creeds? Or should I try to create a synthesis based on academic study, modern thinking and personal faith? My solution, containing both answers and question, is formed in a few narrow lines in this epilogue which tries to fulfil the task of theology, namely, to give rational structures to reality and faith.

The scope of this study has been to analyse historical experiences of God documented in the pages of the Old Testament. We have gone through the ancient beliefs, demands, manipulations, hopes and fears. The whole scale of emotions and passions of oriental man has been used in a theological context: God is described in a very anthropomorphic way. He loves, becomes angry and jealous, sees and feels—just like a man. In many ways Old Testament writers share the concepts of the oriental world where the anger of God is the rule and not the exception. After academic study of the oriental concepts of God it is time to ask: Do we share these points of view at the end of the second millennium CE—after Christ and after the Enlightenment?

Whenever we try to say something about God we enter an area which is not definable in absolute terms but rather deals with human understandings of the absolute. This means that every assumption and belief about God, ancient or modern, is filtered to us through human experiences and interpretations.

In the light of this point of view it is possible to formulate a first thesis about God-talk. All those strivings that have taken God as a part of their own ideological or political programme, so making him a tool or an instrument of their power struggle against other groups, have gone beyond the limits of human competence. Whenever opponents are either annihilated physically (Num. 16–17; Deut. 13; Josh. 7) or mentally and/or physically subordinated (Num. 16–17) human beings have taken the place of God and acted in his name (sic! Josh. 22.19). To say that the right values, doctrines or religious structures are worth protecting should never mean physical or mental violence against theological or ideological dissidents.

My second thesis is related to the unsolved problem of how to speak about justice, power and God. In deuteronomistic theology two preoccupations seem to have priority: God (Yahweh) is the real ruler of the world (instead of political powers or other gods) *and* the same God guarantees the fulfilment of justice on Earth. This combination had a logical consequence in deuteronomistic theology: unhappy historical events and experiences must have been caused by God who in this way had punished human beings. National disaster, exile, happened according to the will of God because he had to punish Israelites for idolatry. This logic means, however, that the powerful God of justice is also automatically the God of revenge and war.

In the case of idolatry still another aspect enters the picture. Caused by the difficult national and religious situation deuteronomistic thinkers (especially DtrN) tried to protect their identity with aggression and polemic against foreign influence. Using the category of 'foreigner' or 'otherness' they labelled especially those people who had defined their concepts about God in a different way. One of the major theological (and ideological) achievements of the deuteronomistic party was to connect Yahweh with exclusive monotheism and intolerance.

Preoccupation with God's rule on Earth and guarantee of justice was reinforced by weak national identity to face and tolerate foreign religious influence which probably raised serious questions related to surviving and maintaining hope for the future. In these circumstances it was inevitable that DtrN would launch a massive programme where exile and idolatry, that is, 'the otherness', was sold to the people as a single unit. Overheated building of religious identity turned to the fight against enemies (real and imaginative), against the foreign and against otherness. The God that deuteronomistic theologians created in their own image was thus the God of strict dogmatism, intolerance and fundamentalism—and of course: the God of anger. To read the deuteronomistic text and ignore this hard reality is to exercise unaware, naive ideological criticism. The intolerance as well as the identity built on such cost to others cannot morally be accepted. My own well-being should not be paid for with the suffering of others.

The influence of deuteronomistic theology was extensive. In the Old Testament this basic model continued until the advent of apocalypticism where the power of God and realization of justice were pushed into the transcendental sphere. The common understanding was that the world can be bad and rotten but God already rules now in heaven and in future will also rule on earth. Similar structures were so widespread within the environment where Christianity was born that we can maintain that apocalyptic ideas worked as a midwife to Christianity.

Do we have any other choices? Is our concept of a strong God fixed firmly or even permanently in the soil of deuteronomistic theology? In the Old Testament there are voices of the (Old Testament marginal?) dissidents like the writers of the books of Jonah, Job and wisdom literature who did not see foreigners as a threat. In the texts of Second Isaiah, in the poems about the Servant of Yahweh, we catch a glimpse of different tones, when Israel is the poor one who suffers and does not hit back. In the Old Testament these ideas stay, however, in the margins.

Finally, the major objection to the overall deuteronomistic structure arises from the Jesus-tradition. Exploration of the fate of Jesus of Nazareth on the cross in the Gospel of Mark and the writings of Paul leads them to build their theology not on the idea of a strong and just God, but on suffering. Both Mark and Paul were convinced that in the events of the cross God had revealed his genuine face: weakness, misery and death were the most effective and authentic revelation of God which was confirmed in the resurrection of Jesus. Thus the gospel of Jesus gives up the need to exert power and to rule. To go further still: the God of the crucified and powerless Jesus cannot be the same as the deuteronomistic God of anger.

However, also in New Testament the stream stressing the power of God seems still to be alive because the Gospel of John gives a rather different description of Jesus. The incarnated *logos* acts and speaks like the representative of power. He is not really a poor sufferer but even on the cross represents a powerful God without showing any sign of weakness.

If such a duality exists even at the core of Christianity can we hope to go further? Where can we explore the true face of God? In the anger of God in exile or in the crucified Jesus of Nazareth? In the powerful Pantocrator or in the crucified man? This basic distinction has been formulated and answered in diverse ways during the long process of interpretation of the Christian faith without any final resolution. Both lines have been represented in the history of interpretation. An eager follower in the line of Mark and Paul was Martin Luther who created a highly sophisticated model of the theology of the cross. His definite answer was that God reveals himself in the weak, in the poor, in the suffering, in the nothing which becomes a new creation by the act of God. Another example, a modern one, comes from Asia, where Dalit theology rewrites and interprets classical Christian tradition from its own contextual perspective, so creating a theology of those who are pushed outside official and social power structures. It is, however, fair to note that not all have come to the same conclusion. The movement wanting to see God as a strong ruler who is still in charge has also had its followers, not least among minor groups of Protestant Christians.

Should we make our choice and carry our flag against those who represent a different opinion? Liberation from old structures is not, however, possible without creating new models where basic motives can be dealt with, by forsaking, agreeing or modifying them. New paths could be opened up if the deeply anthropomorphic concepts of God are reduced to the major theological motive which faces basic questions with which the deuteronomistic theology of anger was concerned: justice, major disasters of life and questions about hope and love.

Reality: Just as in the Old Testament period, the contemporary world still has more or less the same signs of a dark side which led to the model of the anger of God. Even if we do not share the world-view of deuteronomistic theology we have to try to solve the basic questions behind this theology. What can we say about wars, economical depression, social exclusion, and so on?

Impossible: The Old Testament connects God's anger with state affairs, politics, ethics and religious practices in a way that seems confusing to present categories of thought. Deuteronomistic theology underlines how Yahweh protects Israel as an elected nation against other nations but when she forsakes him by worshipping other gods, then Yahweh, ruler of all nations, brings judgment.

At the moment when we give up the particularistic idea that God is only for our group, only for our nation in the whole world, we have also to admit that political issues between the nations cannot be explained in theological terms as attempted in deuteronomistic theology. It is not possible to explain the 1930s Soviet occupation of Estonia and the contrasting 'miracle of Winterwar' in which Finns protected their native soil, by claiming that Estonians were bigger sinners than pious Finns. Nor is it possible to explain the Falklands war or Northern Ireland conflict with Old Testament concepts. These wars must rather be explained in terms of geopolitics and the interests of the superpowers or other political groups.

If this basic assumption is accepted we can go one step further and apply the same principle to smaller communities. It is impossible to say that people belonging to the economically, spiritually, intellectually or culturally hard-pressed areas in north-eastern Finland, East Manchester or anywhere else are bigger sinners, or especially guilty, and that therefore God punishes them. Such a simple Old Testament (especially chronistic) calculation that there is a clear connection between transgression and punishment is not a working model—the reality is simply too complex for it.

Necessity: In human life there is, however, a place for responsibility. In one way or another people or society have to pay for injustice even if there is no clear connection in one's life between reason and event. Injustice is faced and suffered by a single person, by a family, by a community or by a global community. Sooner or later transgressions find a target and somebody pays for it—unfortunately too often somebody from the least guilty part of society, thanks to structural injustice.

Hope over anger: Does God exist in this modern world? Lack of good, lack of responsibilities leads persons, communities and the world to confront the unfortunate side of life. This reality does not exclude God from the world but forces one to take it into the consideration in the process of modifying the concept of God. The basic paradigm in Christian faith is that God, after all, is not somewhere beyond the world but is with the world (especially with the poor, excluded and foreigner), or in the world, and this work of creation confirmed through the resurrection still presents a new hope for life. One of the central paradigms in deuteronomistic theology (DtrH) was that life, land, people around, food, and so on, are a gift from God, totally given by grace without being earned—this theological statement is still worth exploring as a sign of hope in the modern world.

BIBLIOGRAPHY

Ahlström, G.W., 'An Archaeological Picture of Iron Age Religions in Ancient Palestine', *StudOr* 55 (1984), pp. 115-45.
Albertz, R., *A History of Israelite Religion in the Old Testament Period* (2 vols.; OTL; trans. J. Bowden; Louisville, KY: Westminster/John Knox Press, 1994).
Aurelius, E., *Der Fürbitter Israels: Eine Studie zum Mosebild im Alten Testament* (ConBOT, 27; Lund: Almqvist & Wiksell, 1988).
Baloian, B.E., *Anger in the Old Testament* (American University Studies; Theology and Religion, 99; New York: Peter Lang, 1992).
Barrick, W.B., 'On the Meaning of בית־ה/במות and בתי־הבמות and the Composition of the Kings History', *JBL* 115 (1996), pp. 621-42.
Becker, U., *Richterzeit und Königtum: Redaktionsgeschichtliche Studien zum Richterbuch* (BZAW, 192; Berlin: W. de Gruyter, 1990).
Benzinger, I., *Die Bücher der Könige* (KHAT, 9; Freiburg: J.C.B. Mohr, 1899).
Berg, W., 'Die Eifersucht Gottes—ein problematischer Zug des alttestamentlichen Gottesbildes?', *BZ* NS 23 (1979), pp. 197-211.
Blenkinsopp, J., *Gibeon and Israel: The Role of Gibeon and the Gibeonites in the Political and Religious History of Early Israel* (SOTSMS, 2; Cambridge: Cambridge University Press, 1972).
Boling, R.G, *Joshua: A New Translation with Notes and Commentary* (AB, 6; New York: Doubleday, 1982).
Brettler, M.Z., 'Jud 1,1-2,10: From Appendix to Prologue', *ZAW* 101 (1989), pp. 433-35.
Brongers, H.A., 'Der Eifer des Herrn Zebaoth', *VT* 13 (1963), pp. 269-84.
Budde, K., *Die Bücher Richter und Samuel: Ihre Quellen und ihr Aufbau* (Giessen: Ricker, 1890).
Burney, C.F., *The Book of Judges: With Introduction and Notes* (London: Rivingtons, 2nd edn, 1920).
Butler T.C., *Joshua* (WBC, 7; Waco, TX: Word Books, 1983).
Cholewinski, A., *Heiligkeitsgesetz und Deuteronomium: Eine vergleichende Studie* (AnBib, 66; Rome: Biblical Institute Press, 1976).
Clements, R.E., *Deuteronomy* (OTG; Sheffield: Sheffield Academic Press, 1989).
Clines, D.J.A, *Interested Parties: The Ideology of Writers and Readers of the Hebrew Bible* (JSOTSup, 205; Sheffield: Sheffield Academic Press, 1995).
Cowley, A., *Aramaic Papyri of the Fifth Century* (Oxford: Clarendon Press, 1923).
Cross, F.M., *Canaanite Myth and Hebrew Epic: Essays in the History of the Religion of Israel* (Cambridge, MA: Harvard University Press, 2nd edn, 1975).
Dietrich, W., *Prophetie und Geschichte: Eine redaktionsgeschichtliche Untersuchung zum deuteronomistischen Geschichtswerk* (FRLANT, 108; Göttingen: Vandenhoeck & Ruprecht, 1972).

—David, Saul und die Propheten: Das Verhältnis von Religion und Politik nach den prophetischen Überlieferungen vom frühesten Königtum in Israel (BWANT, 122; Stuttgart: W. Kohlhammer, 1987).

Eissfeldt, O., *Hexateuch-Synopse: Die Erzählung der fünf Bücher Mose und des Buches Josua mit dem Anfang des Richterbuches* (repr.; Darmstadt: Wissenschaftliche Buchgesellshaft, 1983).

Elliger, K., *Leviticus* (HAT, 4; Tübingen: J.C.B. Mohr, 1966).

Floss, J.P., *Jahwe dienen—Göttern dienen: Terminologische, literarische und semantische Untersuchung einer theologischen Aussage zum Gottesverhältnis im Alten Testament* (BBB, 45; Bonn: Hanstein, 1975).

Foresti, F., *The Rejection of Saul in the Perspective of the Deuteronomistic School* (Studia Theologica, Teresianum, 5; Rome: Edizioni del Teresianum, 1984).

Fritz, V., *Das Buch Josua* (HAT, 7; Tübingen: J.C.B. Mohr, 1994).

Grabbe, L., *Judaism from Cyrus to Hadrian* (London: SCM Press, 1992).

Görg, M., *Josua* (Die Neue Echter Bibel; Kommentar zum Alten Testament mit der Einheitsübersetzung, 26; Würzburg: Echter Verlag, 1991).

Halbe, J., 'Gibeon und Israel: Art, Veranlassung und Ort der Deutung ihres Verhältnisses in Jos. IX', *VT* 25 (1975), pp. 613-41.

Hayes, J.H., *An Introduction to Old Testament Study* (Nashville: Abingdon Press, 2nd edn, 1980).

Hentschel, G., *2 Könige* (Die Neue Echter Bibel; Kommentar zum Alten Testament mit der Einheitsübersetzung, 11; Stuttgart: Echter Verlag, 1985).

Herrmann, S., 'Die konstruktive Restauration: Das Deuteronomium als Mitte biblischer Theologie', in H.W. Wolff (ed.), *Probleme biblischer Theologie* (Festschrift G. von Rad; Munich: Chr. Kaiser Verlag, 1971), pp. 155-70.

Holmes, S., *Joshua: The Hebrew and Greek Texts* (Cambridge: Cambridge University Press, 1914).

Japhet, S.,*The Ideology of the Book of Chronicles and its Place in Biblical Thought* (BEATAJ, 9; New York: Peter Lang, 1989).

Jepsen, A., *Die Quellen des Königsbuches* (Halle: Max Niemeyer Verlag, 1953).

—'Ahabs Busse: Ein kleiner Beitrag zur Methode literar historischer Einordnung', in A. Kuschke and E. Kutsch (eds.), *Archäologie und Altes Testament* (Festschrift K. Galling; Tübingen: J.C.B. Mohr, 1970), pp. 145-55.

Jones, G.H., *1 and 2 Kings* (2 vols.; NCB; Grand Rapids: Eerdmans; London: Marshall, Morgan & Scott, 1984).

Kaiser, O., *Das Buch des Propheten Jesaja: Kapitel 1–12* (ATD, 17; Göttingen: Vandenhoeck & Ruprecht, 5th rev. edn, 1981).

—*Das Buch des Propheten Jesaja: Kapitel 13–39* (ATD, 18; Göttingen: Vandenhoeck & Ruprecht, 3rd rev. edn, 1983).

—*Einleitung in das Alte Testament: Eine Einführung in ihre Ergebnisse und Probleme* (Gütersloh: Gerd Mohn, 5th edn, 1984).

Keller, C.A., 'שבע ni. schwören', *THAT*, II, pp. 855-63.

Kellermann, D., *Die Priesterschrift von Numeri 1_1 bis 10_{10} literarkritisch und traditionsgeschichtlich untersucht* (BZAW, 120; Berlin: W. de Gruyter, 1970).

Kenyon, K.M., *Archaeology in the Holy Land* (London: Ernest Benn; New York: W.W. Norton, 4th edn, 1979).

Kittel, R., *Die Bücher der Könige* (HKAT, 1.5; Göttingen: Vandenhoeck & Ruprecht, 1900).

Kloppenborg, J.S., 'Joshua 22: The Priestly Editing of an Ancient Tradition', *Bib* 62 (1981), pp. 347-71.
Knapp, D., *Deuteronomium 4: Literarische Analyse und theologische Interpretation* (GTA, 35; Göttingen: Vandenhoeck & Ruprecht, 1987).
Kraeling, E.G., *The Brooklyn Museum Aramaic Papyri: New Documents of Fifth Century B.C. from the Jewish Colony at Elephantine* (London: Oxford University Press, 1953).
Kuenen, A., *Historisch-kritische Einleitung in die Bücher des Alten Testaments*, 1.1 (Leipzig: Schulze, 1887).
—*Historisch-kritische Einleitung in die Bücher des Alten Testaments*, 1.2 (Leipzig: Schulze, 1890).
Latvus, K., *Jumalan viha: Redaktiokriittinen tutkimus Joosuan ja Tuomarien kirjojen jumalakuvasta* (SESJ, 58; Helsinki: Suomen Eksegeettinen Seura, 1993; *The Anger of God: A Redaction Critical View of the Concept of God in the Books of Joshua and Judges* [SESJ, 58; Helsinki: The Finnish Exegetical Society, 1993]).
—'From Army Campsite to Partners in Peace: The Changing Role of the Gibeonites in the Redaction Process of Josh. x 1-8; xi19', in K.-D. Schunk and M. Augustin (eds.), *'Lasset uns Brücken bauen ...': Collected Communications to the XVth Congress of the International Organization for the Study of the Old Testament, Cambridge 1995* (BEATAJ, 42; Frankfurt am Main: Peter Lang, 1998), pp. 111-15.
Levin, C., *Der Sturz der Königin Atalja: Ein Kapitel zur Geschichte Judas im 9. Jahrhundert v. Chr* (SBS, 105; Stuttgart: Verlag Katholisches Bibelwerk, 1982).
—'Joschija im deuteronomistischen Geschichtswerk', *ZAW* 96 (1984), pp. 351-71.
—*Die Verheissung des neuen Bundes in ihrem Theologie geschichtlichen Zusammenhang ausgelegt* (FRLANT, 137; Göttingen: Vandenhoeck & Ruprecht, 1985).
Lindström, F., *God and the Origin of Evil: A Contextual Analysis of Alleged Monistic Evidence in the Old Testament* (ConBOT, 21; Lund: Almqvist & Wiksell, 1983).
Lohfink, N., *Das Hauptgebot: Eine Untersuchung literarischer Einleitungsfragen zu Dtn 5–11* (AnBib, 20; Rome: Pontifico Istituto Biblico, 1963).
—*Die Priesterschrift und die Geschichte* (VTSup, 29; Leiden: E.J. Brill, 1978), pp. 189-225.
López, F. García, 'Analyse littéraire de Deutéronome, V–XI', *RB* 84 (1977), pp. 481-522.
Mayes, A.D.H., *The Story of Israel between Settlement and Exile: A Redactional Study of the Deuteronomistic History* (London: SCM Press, 1983).
—'Deuteronomy 29, Joshua 9, and the Place of the Gibeonites in Israel', in N. Lohfink (ed.), *Deuteronomium: Entsehung, Gestalt und Botschaft* (BETL, 68; Leuven: Leuven University Press, 1985), pp. 321-25.
McCarthy, D.J., 'The Wrath of Yahweh and the Structural Unity of the Deuteronomistic History', in J.L. Crenshaw and J.T. Willis (eds.), *Essays in Old Testament Ethics* (J. Philip Hyatt in Memorium; New York: Ktav, 1974), pp. 97-110.
—*Treaty and Covenant: A Study in Form in the Ancient Oriental Documents and in the Old Testament* (Rome: Pontifical Biblical Institute, new edn completely rewritten, 1978).
McKane, W., *A Critical and Exegetical Commentary on Jeremiah. I. Introduction and Commentary on Jeremiah I–XXV* (ICC; Edinburgh: T. & T. Clark, 1986).
Menes, A., 'Tempel und Synagoge', *ZAW* NS 9 (1932), pp. 268-76.
Minokami, Y., *Die Revolution des Jehu* (GTA, 38; Göttingen: Vandenhoeck & Ruprecht, 1989).

Mittmann, S., *Deuteronomium 11–63 literarkritisch und traditionsgeschichtlich untersucht* (BZAW, 139; Berlin: W. de Gruyter, 1975).

Negev, A. (ed.), *The Archaeological Encyclopedia of the Holy Land* (New York: Prentice Hall Press, 3rd edn, 1990).

Nelson, R., *The Double Redaction of the Deuteronomistic History* (JSOTSup, 18; Sheffield: Sheffield Academic Press, 1981).

Nicholson, E.W., *God and his People: Covenant and Theology in the Old Testament* (Oxford: Clarendon Press, 1986).

Nissinen, M., *Prophetie, Redaktion und Fortschreibung im Hoseabuch: Studien zum Werdegang eines Prophetenbuches im Lichte von Hos 4 und 11* (AOAT, 231; Kevelaer: Butzon & Bercker; Neukirchen–Vluyn: Neukirchener Verlag, 1991).

Noth, M., *Überlieferungsgeschichte des Pentateuch* (Stuttgart: W. Kohlhammer, 1948).

—*Das Buch Josua* (HAT, 7; Tübingen: J.C.B. Mohr, rev. edn, 1953).

—*Das vierte Buch Mose: Numeri* (ATD, 7; Göttingen: Vandenhoeck & Ruprecht, 1966).

—*Überlieferungsgeschichtliche Studien: Die sammelnden und bearbeitenden Geschichtswerke im Alten Testament* (Tübingen: Max Niemeyer Verlag, 3rd edn, 1967).

—*Könige* (BKAT, 9.1; Neukirchen–Vluyn: Neukirchener Verlag, 1968).

Nowack, W., *Richter, Ruth* (HKAT, 1.4.1; Göttingen: Vandenhoeck & Ruprecht, 1900).

Otto, R., *Das Heilige: Über das Irrationale in der Idee des göttlichen und sein Verhältnis zum Rationalen* (Breslau: Trewendt und Granier, 9th edn, 1922).

Ottosson, M., *Josuaboken: En programskrift för davidisk restauration* (Acta Universitatis Upsaliensis; Studia Biblica Upsaliensia, 1; Uppsala: Uppsala Universitet, 1991).

Parpola, S., and K. Watanabe (eds.), *Neo-Assyrian Treaties and Loyalty Oaths* (SAA, 2; Helsinki: Helsinki University Press, 1988).

Peckham, B., *The Composition of the Deuteronomistic History* (HSM, 35; Missoula, MT: Scholars Press, 1985).

Peels, H.G.L., *The Vengeance of God: The Meaning of the Root NQM and the Function of the NQM-Texts in the Context of Divine Revelation in the Old Testament* (OTS, 31; Leiden: E.J. Brill, 1994).

Perlitt, L., *Deuteronomium* (BKAT, 5.2; Neukirchen–Vluyn: Neukirchener Verlag, 1991).

Phillips, A., *Ancient Israel's Criminal Law: A New Approach to the Decalogue* (Oxford: Basil Blackwell, 1970).

Polzin, R., *Moses and the Deuteronomist: A Literary Study of the Deuteronomic History*, I (New York: Seabury, 1980).

Pope, M.H., 'Oath', *IDB*, III, pp. 575-77.

Porten, B., *Archives from Elephantine: The Life of an Ancient Jewish Military Colony* (Berkeley: University of California Press, 1968).

Porten, B., and A. Yardeni, *Textbook of Aramaic Documents from Ancient Egypt. I. Letters* (Jerusalem: Hebrew University, 1986).

Preuss, H.D., *Deuteronomium* (EdF, 164; Darmstadt: Wissenschaftliche Buchgesellschaft, 1982).

Pritchard, J.B., *Gibeon's History in the Light of Excavations* (VTSup, 7; Leiden: E.J. Brill, 1959).

—*Gibeon Where the Sun Stood Still: The Discovery of the Biblical City* (Princeton, NJ: Princeton University Press, 1962).

Provan, I.W., *Hezekiah and the Books of Kings: A Contribution to the Debate about the Composition of the Deuteronomistic History* (BZAW, 172; Berlin: W. de Gruyter, 1988).

—*Lamentations* (NCB; Grand Rapids: Eerdmans, 1991).
Puukko, A.F., *Das Deuteronomium: Eine literarkritische Untersuchung* (Leipzig: J.C. Hinrichs, 1909).
Rad, G. von, *Theologie des Alten Testaments*. I. *Die Theologie der geschichtlichen Überlieferungen Israels* (Munich: Chr. Kaiser Verlag, 8th edn, 1982).
Richter, W., *Die Bearbeitung des 'Retterbuches' in der deuteronomischen Epoche* (BBB, 21; Bonn: Hanstein, 1964).
Ringgren, H., 'Einige Schilderungen des göttlichen Zorns', in E. Würthwein and O. Kaiser (eds.), *Tradition und Situation: Studien zur alttestamentlichen Prophetie* (Festschrift A.Weiser; Göttingen: Vandenhoeck & Ruprecht, 1963), pp. 107-13.
Rofé, A., 'The Laws of Warfare in the Book of Deuteronomy: Their Origin, Intent and Positivity', *JSOT* 32 (1985), pp. 23-44.
Šanda, A., *Die Bücher der Könige I–II* (EHAT, 9.1; Münster: Aschendorff, 1911 [1912]).
Schwienhorst, L., *Die Eroberung Jerichos: Exegetische Untersuchung zu Josua 6* (SBS, 122; Stuttgart: Verlag Katholisches Bibelwerk, 1986).
Smend, R., 'Das Gesetz und die Völker: Ein Beitrag zur deuteronomistischen Redaktionsgeschichte', in H.W. Wolff (ed.), *Probleme biblischer Theologie* (Festschrift G. von Rad; Munich: Chr. Kaiser Verlag, 1971), pp. 494-509.
—*Die Entstehung des Alten Testaments* (ThW, 1; Stuttgart: W. Kohlhammer, 2nd rev. edn, 1981).
Smith, M., *Palestinian Parties and Politics that Shaped the Old Testament* (New York: Columbia University Press, 1971).
Soggin, J.A., *Joshua: A Commentary* (OTL; London: SCM Press, 1972).
—*Judges: A Commentary* (OTL; London: SCM Press, 1981).
Spieckermann, H., *Juda unter Assur in der Sargonidenzeit* (FRLANT, 129; Göttingen: Vandenhoeck & Ruprecht, 1982).
—'Barmherzig und gnädig ist der Herr . . . ', *ZAW* 102 (1990), pp. 1-18.
Stade, B., 'Zur Entstehungsgeschichte des vordeuteronomistischen Richterbuches', *ZAW* 1 (1881), pp. 339-43.
Stade, B., and F. Schwally, *The Books of Kings: Critical Edition of the Hebrew Text* (SBOT, 9; Leipzig: J.C. Hinrichs, 1904).
Stemberger, G., *Das klassische Judentum: Kultur und Geschichte der rabbinischen Zeit 70 n. Chr.–1040 n. Chr.* (Munich: C.H. Beck, 1979).
Steuernagel, C., *Das Deuteronomium: Das Buch Josua* (HKAT, 1.3; Göttingen: Vandenhoeck & Ruprecht, 1900).
—*Lehrbuch der Einleitung in das Alte Testament* (Tübingen: J.C.B. Mohr, 1912).
—*Das Deuteronomium: Das Buch Josua* (HKAT, 1.3; Göttingen: Vandenhoeck & Ruprecht, 2nd edn, 1923).
Stolz, F., 'Monotheismus in Israel', in O. Keel (ed.), *Monotheismus im Alten Israel und seiner Umwelt* (Biblische Beiträge, 14; Freiburg: Katholisches Bibelwerk, 1980), pp. 143-84.
Thiel, W., 'Erwägungen zum Alter des Heiligkeitsgesetzes', *ZAW* 81 (1969), pp. 40-73.
Tov, E., *Textual Criticism of the Hebrew Bible* (Minneapolis: Fortress Press; Assen: Van Gorcum, 1992).
Trebolle Barrera J., 'Textual Variants in 4QJudg[a] and the Textual and Editorial History of the Book of Judges', *RevQ* 54 (1989), pp. 229-45.

Ulrich E., F.M. Cross, S.W. Crawford, J.S. Duncan, P.W. Skehan, E. Tov and J.T. Barrera, *Qumran Cave 4, IX Deuteronomy, Joshua, Judges, Kings* (DJD, 14; Oxford: Clarendon Press, 1995).

Veijola, T., *Die ewige Dynastie: David und die Entstehung seiner Dynastie nach der deuteronomistischen Darstellung* (AASF, Series B, 193; Helsinki: Academia Scientiarum Fennica, 1975).

—*Das Königtum in der Beurteilung der deuteronomistischen Historiographie: Eine redaktionsgeschichtliche Untersuchung* (AASF, Series B; Helsinki: Academia Scientiarum Fennica, 1977).

—*Verheissung in der Krise: Studien zur Literatur und Theologie der Exilzeit anhand des 89: Psalms* (AASF, Series B, 220; Helsinki: Academia Scientiarum Fennica, 1982).

—'Das Klagebet in Literatur und Leben der Exilsgeneration am Beispiel einiger Prosatexte' in J.A. Emerton (ed.), *Congress Volume: Salamanca 1983* (VTSup, 36; Leiden: E.J. Brill, 1985), pp. 286-307.

—'Wahrheit und Intoleranz nach Deuteronomium 13', *ZTK* 92 (1995), pp. 287-314.

—'Bundestheologische Redaktion im Deuteronomium', in T. Veijola (ed.), *Das Deuteronomium und seine Querbeziehungen* (SESJ, 62; Helsinki: Finnische Exegetische Gesellschaft; Göttingen: Vandenhoeck & Ruprecht, 1996), pp. 242-76.

Vink, J.G., 'The Date and Origin of the Priestly Code in the Old Testament', *OTS* 15 (1969), pp. 1-144.

Volz, P., *Das Dämonische in Jahwe* (Tübingen: J.C.B. Mohr, 1924).

Vorländer, H., 'Der Monotheismus Israels als Antwort auf die Krise des Exils', in Bernhard Lang (ed.), *Der einzige Gott: Die Geburt des biblischen Monotheismus* (Munich: Kösel Verlag, 1981), pp. 84-114.

Wellhausen, J., *Die Composition des Hexateuchs und der historischen Bücher des Alten Testaments* (Berlin: George Reimer, 3rd edn, 1899).

Westermann, C., 'Boten des Zorns: Der Begriff des Zornes Gottes in der Prophetie', in J. Jeremias and L. Perlitt (eds.), *Die Botschaft und die Boten* (Festschrift H.W. Wolff; Neukirchen–Vluyn: Neukirchener Verlag, 1981), pp. 147-56.

Wette, W.M.L. de, *Dissertatio critico-exegetica qua Deuteronomium a prioribus Pentateuchi libris diversum, alius cuiusdam recentioris auctoris opus esse monstratur* (Jena, 1805).

—*Beiträge zur Einleitung in das Alte Testament* (Halle, 1806/1807; repr.; Darmstadt: Wissenschaftliche Buchgesellschaft, 1971).

Winter, U., *Frau und Göttin: Exegetische und ikonographische Studien zum weiblichen Gottesbild im Alten Israel und in dessen Umwelt* (OBO, 53; Göttingen: Vandenhoeck & Ruprecht, 1983).

Würthwein, E., *Die Bücher der Könige: 1. Kön. 17–2. Kön. 25* (ATD, 11.2; Göttingen: Vandenhoeck & Ruprecht, 1984).

—*Die Bücher der Könige: 1. Kön. 1–16* (ATD, 11.1; Göttingen: Vandenhoeck & Ruprecht, rev. edn, 1985).

Zimmerli, W., *Ezechiel* (BKAT, 13.1-2; Neukirchen–Vluyn: Neukirchener Verlag, 1969).

INDEXES

INDEX OF REFERENCES

Old Testament
Genesis
18.30	26
18.32	26
26.5	56
34.9	34
36.43	56

Exodus
4.14	26
4.24	21
11.8	26
15.7	26
16.22	65
22.23	26
32.10	26
32.11	26
32.12	26
32.22	26
34.31	65
35.27	65

Leviticus
5.15	49
5.21	49
9	79
10.1-7	79
10.3	79
10.6-7	79
10.6	77, 79, 80
10.16	25
14.34	56
18.30	56
22.9	56
25.24	56
26	31, 78
26.1-2	78
26.3-13	78
26.16-39	78
26.21	78
26.23	78
26.24	78
26.27-33	78
26.27	78
26.28	77, 78
26.40	49
26.41	78
27.21	50
27.28	50

Numbers
1.48-54	79, 80
1.51	80
1.53	65, 70, 77, 79, 80
3.7	56
3.28	56
3.32	56
3.38	56
4.32	65
5.6	49
5.12	49
5.27	49
8.26	56
8.35	56
9.19	56
9.23	56
11.1	26
11.10	26
11.33	26
12.9	26
16–17	81-83, 90
16.1-2	82
16.2	65
16.3-7	82
16.3	82
16.7	83
16.8-11	83
16.11	83
16.12-15	82
16.15	82
16.16-17	83
16.18	82
16.19-24	82, 83
16.22	25, 77, 82, 83
16.25-26	82
16.27-34	82
16.27	82
16.32	82, 83
16.35	82
17	84
17.1-5	83
17.6-15	82
17.11	26, 77, 82
18.1-7	79, 80
18.3	56
18.4-5	79
18.4	56
18.5	56, 65, 70, 77, 79, 81
18.7	83
18.14	50

22.22	26	10.12	76	32.21	73
25.3	26	10.15	76	32.22	73
25.4	26	10.18	76		
31.13	65	11.1	56, 76	*Joshua*	
32	55, 57	11.13	76	1	56
32.2	65	11.16-17	43	1.1-2	28, 56, 85
32.10	26	11.17	26, 73		
32.13	26	11.22	76	1.1	54
32.14	26	11.24-25	28	1.2	33
35.28	56	12	58, 62	1.3-6	28, 56, 85
		12.31	26, 73		
Deuteronomy		13	53, 90	1.7	28, 56
1.27	26, 71	13.3	34	1.8-9	28, 56, 86
1.34	25, 71	13.4	76		
1.37	25, 73	13.7	34	1.10-11	28, 56, 85
3.12-20	55	13.14	34		
3.18-20	57	13.17-18	49	1.12-18	28, 55-57, 86
3.24	71	13.18	26, 73		
3.26	26	15.16	76	1.15	54
4.21	25, 73	16.22	26, 73	2.10	85
4.24	40	17.2	34	3.6	16
4.25	25, 73	17.3	34	6–7	50
4.37	76	19.9	76	6	48, 66
5.9	40	20.10-18	66	6.18-19	50
5.10	76	20.16-17	67	6.21	19
6.5	74, 76	20.17-18	49	6.24	19
6.12-15	38	23.6	76	6.26	19
6.14-15	43	28	31, 78	7–8	66
6.14	38	28.14	34	7	47, 48, 50, 51, 53, 54, 88, 90
6.15	26, 40, 73	28.36	34		
		28.64	34		
7.1-2	68	29.19	73		
7.3	34	29.22	26, 73	7.1	26, 48-51, 56, 86
7.4	26, 34, 43, 73	29.23	26, 73		
		29.25	34		
7.8	76	29.26	26, 73	7.2-5	48, 51, 85
7.9	76	29.27	26, 73		
7.13	76	30.6	76	7.6-26	48-51
7.26	49	30.16	76	7.6	50
8.19-20	43	30.17	34	7.7-9	48
8.19	34	30.20	76	7.9-26	86
9.7	25, 73	31.6-7	28	7.13	49
9.8	25, 73	31.17	26, 73	7.18	49, 56
9.18	25, 73	31.20	34	7.19	49
9.19	25, 73	31.29	25, 73	7.26	26
9.20	25, 73	32.5	49	8	48
9.22	25, 73	32.16	25, 73	8.1-29	85
9.28	26, 73	32.19	73	8.1	51

8.31	31, 34	19.1	49, 56	22.32	65		
9	64, 66, 67, 69, 70, 77, 80, 83, 84, 86	19.24	49, 56	23	16, 28, 29, 31-35, 40, 53, 76		
		19.40	49, 56				
		21	29				
		21.43-45	28, 29, 32-34, 36, 39, 85	23.1-5	31-33, 85		
9.1-2	66			23.1-2	29, 30		
9.3-6	66			23.2-4	29, 30		
9.4	64	21.44–23.9	29	23.5	29-31		
9.6-8	66	21.44–23.1	29	23.6-9	32-34		
9.6	66	21.44	32, 38	23.6-8	29-31		
9.8	66	21.45–23.14	29	23.6	32		
9.9-13	64	22	28, 29, 54, 55, 61, 62, 64, 65, 70, 77, 80, 83, 84, 86	23.9-10	30, 32, 33, 85		
9.11	66			23.9	31, 32		
9.12-13	66			23.11-13	29, 30, 32-34		
9.14	65, 66, 68			23.11	32		
9.15	65, 66, 68						
9.16-17	66	22.1-8	54, 55	23.13	32		
9.16	66	22.1-5	57	23.14	30, 32, 85		
9.17	66	22.1-4	55, 56, 86				
9.18-21	65, 66			23.15-16	30, 32-34		
9.18	68, 70	22.2-3	55				
9.20	64	22.3	56	23.15	32		
9.21	69	22.4	56	23.16	26, 32-35		
9.22-27	64	22.5	55, 86				
9.22-23	66	22.6	55, 56, 86	23.20	40		
9.23	66, 69			24	28, 33, 36, 39, 85		
9.24-26	66	22.7-8	55, 57				
10	67	22.7	55				
10.1-2	67	22.9-34	55, 57, 58, 60, 61	24.2	34		
10.1	85			24.13	29		
10.3-4	85			24.16	34		
10.4	67	22.9	56	24.19	40		
10.5-6	67	22.11	61				
10.5	85	22.12	63	*Judges*			
10.7-43	85	22.14	65	1.1–2.5	13		
11.16-20	33	22.16	49	1.13	42		
11.19	67	22.18	25, 54	2–3	44		
13.15	49, 56	22.19	56, 63, 90	2	36, 37, 40, 41, 43, 44, 86		
13.24	49, 56						
15.1	49, 56	22.20	49, 54, 62, 65, 70				
15.17	42			2.7-11	39, 85		
15.21	49, 56			2.7-10	36		
17.1	49, 56	22.24-28	58	2.8-12	39		
17.4	65	22.30	65				
18.21	49, 56	22.31	49	2.11-23	36		

2.11-19	42, 43	10.7-9	43, 45	11.9-11	43
2.11-14	39	10.7	26, 43-	11.9	25, 73
2.11-13	36, 38, 43		45	14.9-10	43
		10.8-9	45	14.9	25, 72
2.11	43	10.8	44	14.15	25, 73
2.12-14	43	10.9	44	15.30	25, 73
2.12-13	43	10.10	43, 44	16.2	25, 72
2.12	25, 36, 38, 39, 43	10.12-14	43	16.7	25, 73
		10.13	34, 43	16.13	25
		10.16	43, 87	16.26	25, 72
2.13-14	39	10.17-18	45, 46, 85	16.33	25, 72
2.13	43			21.22	25, 72
2.14-16	39, 85	10.17	45	22.54	25, 72
2.14-15	43	11	43		
2.14	26, 36, 38, 43	11.1-40	46, 85	*2 Kings*	
		17–21	13	3.27	65, 70
2.15	39, 85			10.20	49
2.16-18	39, 43	*1 Samuel*		13.3	26, 73
2.16	36, 43	1.6	25	14.6	31, 34
2.17	37	1.7	25	17	85
2.18	36, 37, 39, 46, 85, 87	3.11-14	19	17.11	25, 73
		7.1	49	17.17	25, 73
		8.8	34	17.18	25, 73
2.19-23	37	15	19	17.35	34
2.19-21	39	18.21	34	18.12	34
2.20	26, 34, 36, 39	18.23	34	21.6	25, 73
		18.26	34	21.15	25, 73
2.22-23	39	18.27	34	22.13	26, 73
2.22	37, 39	20.34	26	22.17	25, 26, 73
2.23	39	26.19	34		
3	16, 43, 44	28	19	22.26	73
		28.17-19	19	23.19	25, 72
3.6	16	28.18	26, 72	23.26	25, 26
3.7-11	41-44			24–25	85
3.7-8	44, 46	*2 Samuel*		24.20	73, 74
3.7	43, 85	6.7	21, 26, 72		
3.8-11	85			*1 Chronicles*	
3.8	26, 43	21–24	13	2.7	49
3.9	43	22.8	26	5.25	49
3.10	43	24.1	21, 26, 72	10.13	49
6.7-10	46			13.10	26
6.39	26			23.32	56
10	43	*1 Kings*			
10.1-5	46, 85	2.3	56		
10.3-5	45	8.46	25, 73, 74, 79	*2 Chronicles*	
10.5	45			6.36	25
10.6-16	41-46	8.64	49	12.2	49
10.6	43-45	9.6	34	18.1	34

19.2	26	*Job*		54.8	26
19.10	65, 70	20.23	26	54.9	25
24.18	65, 70	42.7	26	56–66	53
25.10	26			57.16	25
25.15	26	*Psalms*		57.17	25
26.16	49	1	28	60.10	26
26.18	49	2.5	26	61.8	26
28.11	26	2.12	25	64.4	25
28.13	26	5.6	26	64.8	25
28.19	49	11.5	26	65.3	25
28.22	49	18.8	26		
28.25	25	19	28	*Jeremiah*	
29.6	49	38.2	26	4.8	26
29.8	26	58.10	26	4.26	26
29.10	26	60.3	25	7.18	25
30.7	49	69.25	26	7.19	25
30.8	26	78.49	26	8.19	25
32.25	65, 70	78.58	25	10.10	26
32.26	26	79.5	25	11.7	25
33.6	25	85.4	26	11.10	34
34.25	25	85.6	25	12.8	26
36.14	49	88.17	26	12.13	26
		101.3	26	13.10	34
Ezra		102.11	26	16.11	34
9–10	53, 60	106.29	25	16.13	34
9	34	106.32	26	21.5	26
9.1-15	50	106.40	26	22.9	34
9.14	25, 34	119	28	25.6	25, 34
10.1-17	50			25.7	25
10.2-4	50	*Proverbs*		25.37	26
10.2	49, 50	6.16	26	25.38	26
10.10	49, 50	16.10	49	28	69
10.11	49			30.24	26
10.14	26, 50	*Ecclesiastes*		32.29	25
		5.5	25	32.30	25
Nehemiah		5.16	26	32.32	25
1.8	49			32.37	26
3.7	69	*Isaiah*		35.15	34
3.37	25	1.14	26	44.3	25, 34
8.1	31, 34	5.25	26	44.4	26
12.45	56	7.4	26	44.8	25
13.2	49	12.1	25	49.37	26
13.18	26	13.9	26	50.13	26
		13.13	26	51.45	26
Esther		19.18-22	60		
1.18	26	34.2	26	*Lamentations*	
		40–55	53	1.12	26, 35
		47.6	25	2.1	35

2.2	35	*Hosea*		*Malachi*	
2.3	26, 35	8.5	26	1.3	26
2.6	35	9.15	26	2.16	26
2.21	35	11.9	26	3.14	56
2.22	35	12.15	25		
3.1	35			Apocrypha	
3.43	35	*Amos*		*1 Maccabees*	
4.11	26, 35	5.21	26	1.64	70
5.22	25, 35	6.8	26		
				2 Maccabees	
Ezekiel		*Jonah*		6.2	59
7.12	26	3.9	26		
7.14	26			New Testament	
8.17	25	*Nahum*		*Matthew*	
14.13	49	1.6	26	3.7	70
15.8	49				
16.26	25	*Habakkuk*		*Acts*	
16.42	25	3.8	26	11.29	57
17.20	49				
18.24	49	*Zephaniah*		*Galatians*	
20.27	49	2.2	26	2.10	57
32.9	25	3.8	26		
39.23	49			*1 Thessalonians*	
39.26	49	*Zechariah*		1.10	70
44.8	56	1.2	25	2.16	70
44.15	56	1.12	26	5.9	70
44.16	56	1.15	25, 26		
44.29	50	3.7	56	Other Ancient	
48.11	56	7.12	26	References	
		8.14	25	Josephus	
Daniel		8.17	26	*Ant.*	
9.7	49	10.3	26	12.9	59
				13.3	59

INDEX OF AUTHORS

Ahlström, G.W. 69
Albertz, R. 52, 57, 81-84
Augustin, M. 67
Aurelius, E. 73, 79, 82, 83

Baloian, B.E. 23, 24
Barrick, W.B. 28
Becker, U. 20, 36-39, 42, 44
Benzinger, I. 14
Berg, W. 23
Blenkinsopp, J. 69
Boling, R.G. 33
Brettler, M.Z. 36
Brongers, H.A. 23
Budde, K. 15, 37
Burney, C.F. 42
Butler, T.C. 31, 33

Cholewinski, A. 78
Clements, R.E. 75
Clines, D.J.A. 64
Cowley, A. 59
Crenshaw, J.L. 22
Cross, F.M. 14, 17, 18

Dietrich, W. 18, 19, 72

Eissfeldt, O. 15, 82, 83
Elliger, K. 78
Emerton, J.A. 48

Floss, J.P. 42
Foresti, F. 72
Fritz, V. 33, 55

García López, F. 43
Görg, M. 28, 63, 66
Grabbe, L. 52, 59

Halbe, J. 65, 66
Hayes, J.H. 15
Hentschel, G. 73
Herrmann, S. 75
Holmes, S. 33
Hölscher, G. 15
Hyatt, J.P. 22

Japhet, S. 41
Jepsen, A. 16, 17
Jeremias, J. 22
Jones, G.H. 72, 73

Kaiser, O. 22, 60, 75, 77
Kellermann, D. 80
Kenyon, K.M. 69
Kittel, R. 14, 72
Kloppenborg, J.S. 55, 58
Knapp, D. 73
Kraeling, E.G. 59, 60
Kuenen, A. 12-16, 20, 37, 55, 65
Kuschke, A. 73
Kutsch, E. 73

Lang, B. 59
Latvus, K. 67, 73
Levin, C. 7, 20
Lindström, F. 23
Lohfink, N. 65, 73, 79

Mayes, A.D.H. 18, 36, 37, 42, 44, 55, 65, 68, 73
McCarthy, D.J. 22, 30
McKane, W. 20
Menes, A. 61
Minokami, Y. 49
Mittmann, S. 71, 73

Nelson, R. 14, 18, 29, 73
Nicholson, E.W. 30
Nissinen, M. 84
Noth, M. 14, 16, 17, 20, 29, 33, 42, 48, 55, 56, 65, 77, 79-83
Nowack, W. 15, 37, 42

Otto, R. 21, 22
Ottosson, M. 66

Parpola, S. 30
Peels, H.G.L. 23, 64
Perlitt, L. 7, 22, 71, 73
Phillips, A. 68
Polzin, R. 51
Pope, M.H. 68
Porten, B. 59
Preuss, H.D. 34, 71, 75
Pritchard, J.B. 69
Provan, I.W. 18
Puukko, A.F. 72

Rad, G. von 41, 74, 75, 83
Richter, W. 37
Ringgren, H. 22
Rofé, A. 67

Sanda, A. 15, 73
Schunk, K.-D. 67
Schwally, F. 72

Schwienhorst, L. 19
Smend, R. 7, 15, 18, 19, 29, 34, 36, 37, 42, 55, 65, 77, 81, 82
Smith, M. 47
Soggin, J.A. 42, 66, 69
Spieckermann, H. 7, 36, 42, 44, 72, 76
Stade, B. 42, 72
Stemberger, G. 61
Steuernagel, C. 15, 16, 55, 63, 65, 71, 73, 74
Stolz, F. 59

Thiel, W. 79
Tov, E. 33, 54
Trebolle Barrera, J. 46

Ulrich, E. 46

Veijola, T. 7, 18-20, 29, 34, 42, 44, 45, 48, 50, 51, 53, 72, 73, 84
Vink, J.G. 61
Volz, P. 21, 22
Vorländer, H. 59

Watanabe, K. 30
Weiser, A. 22
Wellhausen, J. 12, 13, 42, 55, 82
Westermann, C. 22
Wette, W.M.L. de 12
Willis, J.T. 22
Winter, U. 60
Wolff, H.W. 18, 22, 75
Würthwein, E. 14, 19, 20, 22, 34, 49, 72, 73

Yardeni, A. 59

Zimmerli, W. 20

JOURNAL FOR THE STUDY OF THE OLD TESTAMENT
SUPPLEMENT SERIES

173   M. Patrick Graham, William P. Brown and Jeffrey K. Kuan (eds.), *History and Interpretation: Essays in Honour of John H. Hayes*
174   Joe M. Sprinkle, *'The Book of the Covenant': A Literary Approach*
175   Tamara C. Eskenazi and Kent H. Richards (eds.), *Second Temple Studies. II. Temple and Community in the Persian Period*
176   Gershon Brin, *Studies in Biblical Law: From the Hebrew Bible to the Dead Sea Scrolls*
177   David Allan Dawson, *Text-Linguistics and Biblical Hebrew*
178   Martin Ravndal Hauge, *Between Sheol and Temple: Motif Structure and Function in the I-Psalms*
179   J.G. McConville and J.G. Millar, *Time and Place in Deuteronomy*
180   Richard L. Schultz, *The Search for Quotation: Verbal Parallels in the Prophets*
181   Bernard M. Levinson (ed.), *Theory and Method in Biblical and Cuneiform Law: Revision, Interpolation and Development*
182   Steven L. McKenzie and M. Patrick Graham (eds.), *The History of Israel's Traditions: The Heritage of Martin Noth*
183   John Day (ed.), *Lectures on the Religion of the Semites (Second and Third Series) by William Robertson Smith*
184   John C. Reeves and John Kampen (eds.), *Pursuing the Text: Studies in Honor of Ben Zion Wacholder on the Occasion of his Seventieth Birthday*
185   Seth Daniel Kunin, *The Logic of Incest: A Structuralist Analysis of Hebrew Mythology*
186   Linda Day, *Three Faces of a Queen: Characterization in the Books of Esther*
187   Charles V. Dorothy, *The Books of Esther: Structure, Genre and Textual Integrity*
188   Robert H. O'Connell, *Concentricity and Continuity: The Literary Structure of Isaiah*
189   William Johnstone (ed.), *William Robertson Smith: Essays in Reassessment*
190   Steven W. Holloway and Lowell K. Handy (eds.), *The Pitcher is Broken: Memorial Essays for Gösta W. Ahlström*
191   Magne Sæbø, *On the Way to Canon: Creative Tradition History in the Old Testament*
192   Henning Graf Reventlow and William Farmer (eds.), *Biblical Studies and the Shifting of Paradigms, 1850–1914*
193   Brooks Schramm, *The Opponents of Third Isaiah: Reconstructing the Cultic History of the Restoration*
194   Else Kragelund Holt, *Prophesying the Past: The Use of Israel's History in the Book of Hosea*

195	Jon Davies, Graham Harvey and Wilfred G.E. Watson (eds.), *Words Remembered, Texts Renewed: Essays in Honour of John F.A. Sawyer*
196	Joel S. Kaminsky, *Corporate Responsibility in the Hebrew Bible*
197	William M. Schniedewind, *The Word of God in Transition: From Prophet to Exegete in the Second Temple Period*
198	T.J. Meadowcroft, *Aramaic Daniel and Greek Daniel: A Literary Comparison*
199	J.H. Eaton, *Psalms of the Way and the Kingdom: A Conference with the Commentators*
200	Mark Daniel Carroll R., David J.A. Clines and Philip R. Davies (eds.), *The Bible in Human Society: Essays in Honour of John Rogerson*
201	John W. Rogerson, *The Bible and Criticism in Victorian Britain: Profiles of F.D. Maurice and William Robertson Smith*
202	Nanette Stahl, *Law and Liminality in the Bible*
203	Jill M. Munro, *Spikenard and Saffron: The Imagery of the Song of Songs*
204	Philip R. Davies, *Whose Bible Is It Anyway?*
205	David J.A. Clines, *Interested Parties: The Ideology of Writers and Readers of the Hebrew Bible*
206	Møgens Müller, *The First Bible of the Church: A Plea for the Septuagint*
207	John W. Rogerson, Margaret Davies and Mark Daniel Carroll R. (eds.), *The Bible in Ethics: The Second Sheffield Colloquium*
208	Beverly J. Stratton, *Out of Eden: Reading, Rhetoric, and Ideology in Genesis 2–3*
209	Patricia Dutcher-Walls, *Narrative Art, Political Rhetoric: The Case of Athaliah and Joash*
210	Jacques Berlinerblau, *The Vow and the 'Popular Religious Groups' of Ancient Israel: A Philological and Sociological Inquiry*
211	Brian E. Kelly, *Retribution and Eschatology in Chronicles*
212	Yvonne Sherwood, *The Prostitute and the Prophet: Hosea's Marriage in Literary-Theoretical Perspective*
213	Yair Hoffman, *A Blemished Perfection: The Book of Job in Context*
214	Roy F. Melugin and Marvin A. Sweeney (eds.), *New Visions of Isaiah*
215	J. Cheryl Exum, *Plotted, Shot and Painted: Cultural Representations of Biblical Women*
216	Judith E. McKinlay, *Gendering Wisdom the Host: Biblical Invitations to Eat and Drink*
217	Jerome F.D. Creach, *Yahweh as Refuge and the Editing of the Hebrew Psalter*
218	Gregory Glazov, *The Bridling of the Tongue and the Opening of the Mouth in Biblical Prophecy*
219	Gerald Morris, *Prophecy, Poetry and Hosea*
220	Raymond F. Person, Jr, *In Conversation with Jonah: Conversation Analysis, Literary Criticism, and the Book of Jonah*
221	Gillian Keys, *The Wages of Sin: A Reappraisal of the 'Succession Narrative'*
222	R.N. Whybray, *Reading the Psalms as a Book*
223	Scott B. Noegel, *Janus Parallelism in the Book of Job*

224 Paul J. Kissling, *Reliable Characters in the Primary History: Profiles of Moses, Joshua, Elijah and Elisha*
225 Richard D. Weis and David M. Carr (eds.), *A Gift of God in Due Season: Essays on Scripture and Community in Honor of James A. Sanders*
226 Lori L. Rowlett, *Joshua and the Rhetoric of Violence: A New Historicist Analysis*
227 John F.A. Sawyer (ed.), *Reading Leviticus: Responses to Mary Douglas*
228 Volkmar Fritz and Philip R. Davies (eds.), *The Origins of the Ancient Israelite States*
229 Stephen Breck Reid (ed.), *Prophets and Paradigms: Essays in Honor of Gene M. Tucker*
230 Kevin J. Cathcart and Michael Maher (eds.), *Targumic and Cognate Studies: Essays in Honour of Martin McNamara*
231 Weston W. Fields, *Sodom and Gomorrah: History and Motif in Biblical Narrative*
232 Tilde Binger, *Asherah: Goddesses in Ugarit, Israel and the Old Testament*
233 Michael D. Goulder, *The Psalms of Asaph and the Pentateuch: Studies in the Psalter, III*
234 Ken Stone, *Sex, Honor, and Power in the Deuteronomistic History*
235 James W. Watts and Paul House (eds.), *Forming Prophetic Literature: Essays on Isaiah and the Twelve in Honor of John D.W. Watts*
236 Thomas M. Bolin, *Freedom beyond Forgiveness: The Book of Jonah Re-Examined*
237 Neil Asher Silberman and David B. Small (eds.), *The Archaeology of Israel: Constructing the Past, Interpreting the Present*
238 M. Patrick Graham, Kenneth G. Hoglund and Steven L. McKenzie (eds.), *The Chronicler as Historian*
239 Mark S. Smith, *The Pilgrimage Pattern in Exodus* (with contributions by Elizabeth M. Bloch-Smith)
240 Eugene E. Carpenter (ed.), *A Biblical Itinerary: In Search of Method, Form and Content. Essays in Honor of George W. Coats*
241 Robert Karl Gnuse, *No Other Gods: Emergent Monotheism in Israel*
242 K.L. Noll, *The Faces of David*
243 Henning Graf Reventlow, *Eschatology in the Bible and in Jewish and Christian Tradition*
244 Walter E. Aufrecht, Neil A. Mirau and Steven W. Gauley (eds.), *Aspects of Urbanism in Antiquity: From Mesopotamia to Crete*
245 Lester L. Grabbe, *Can a 'History of Israel' Be Written?*
246 Gillian M. Bediako, *Primal Religion and the Bible: William Robertson Smith and his Heritage*
248 Etienne Nodet, *A Search for the Origins of Judaism: From Joshua to the Mishnah*
249 William Paul Griffin, *The God of the Prophets: An Analysis of Divine Action*
250 Josette Elayi and Jean Sapin (eds.), *Beyond the River: New Perspectives on Transeuphratene*

251 Flemming A.J. Nielsen, *The Tragedy in History: Herodotus and the Deuteronomistic History*
252 David C. Mitchell, *The Message of the Psalter: An Eschatological Programme in the Book of Psalms*
253 William Johnstone, *1 and 2 Chronicles, Vol. 1: 1 Chronicles 1–2 Chronicles 9: Israel's Place among the Nations*
254 William Johnstone, *1 and 2 Chronicles, Vol. 2: 2 Chronicles 10–36: Guilt and Atonement*
255 Larry L. Lyke, *King David with the Wise Woman of Tekoa: The Resonance of Tradition in Parabolic Narrative*
256 Roland Meynet, *Rhetorical Analysis: An Introduction to Biblical Rhetoric* translated by Luc Racaut
257 Philip R. Davies and David J.A. Clines (eds.), *The World of Genesis: Persons, Places, Perspectives*
258 Michael D. Goulder, *The Psalms of the Return (Book V, Psalms 107–150): Studies in the Psalter, IV*
259 Allen Rosengren Petersen, *The Royal God: Enthronement Festivals in Ancient Israel and Ugarit?*
260 A.R. Pete Diamond, Kathleen M. O'Connor and Louis Stulman (eds.) *Trouble with Jeremiah: Prophecy in Conflict*
262 Victor H. Matthews, Bernard M. Levinson and Tikva Frymer-Kensky (eds.), *Gender and Law in the Hebrew Bible and the Ancient Near East*
264 Donald F. Murray, *Divine Prerogative and Royal Pretension: Pragmatics, Poetics and Polemics in a Narrative Sequence about David (2 Samuel 5.17–7.29)*
266 Cheryl Exum and Stephen D. Moore (eds.), *Biblical Studies/Cultural Studies: The Third Sheffield Colloquium*
269 David J.A. Clines and Stephen D. Moore (eds.), *Auguries: The Jubilee Volume of the Sheffield Department of Biblical Studies*
270 John Day (ed.), *King and Messiah in Israel and the Ancient Near East: Proceedings of the Oxford Old Testament Seminar*
272 James Richard Linville, *Israel in the Book of Kings: The Past as a Project of Social Identity*
273 Meir Lubetski, Claire Gottlieb and Sharon Keller (eds.), *Boundaries of the Ancient Near Eastern World: A Tribute to Cyrus H. Gordon*
276 Raz Kletter, *Economic Keystones: The Weight System of the Kingdom of Judah*
277 Augustine Pagolu, *The Religion of the Patriarchs*
278 Lester L. Grabbe (ed.), *Leading Captivity Captive: 'The Exile' as History and Ideology*
291 Christine Schams, *Jewish Scribes in the Second-Temple Period*
292 David J.A. Clines, *On the Way to the Postmodern: Old Testament Essays, 1967–1998 Volume 1*
293 David J.A. Clines, *On the Way to the Postmodern: Old Testament Essays, 1967–1998 Volume 2*